A Teacher's Guide for My Generations

A Course in Jewish Family History

Dr. Alan A. Kay

BEHRMAN HOUS

For my mother and father,
Rose and Milton Kay,
who kindled the light
and whose love and support
keep it burning

Acknowledgements

I am grateful to my friend and colleague Arthur Kurzweil for his confidence in me and for his respect for my commitment to Jewish education.

A.A.K.

ISBN 0-87441-384-2

MANUFACTURED IN THE UNITED STATES OF AMERICA

CONTENTS

ORIENTATION

Family history and genealogy have always been important in Jewish tradition. Beginning with the Torah—where hardly a figure is introduced without some identification of his or her family history—the idea of "m'dor l'dor" ("from generation to generation") has been fundamental to Jewish consciousness.

Family history can bridge the seven continents of Jewish ideas: 1) the uniqueness of the individual; 2) the life cycle events which deepen our understanding of the Jewish way of life and death; 3) the continuity of generations reflected in one's own family history; 4) the continuity of generations reflected in the history of the Jewish people; 5) Torah; 6) tradition; 7) mitzvot.

Genealogy begins with the study of one's *own* history, and since one's own history is always in the making, students of genealogy and family history become actively engaged as their own historians as well as record-keepers for their families. In a broader sense, family history encompasses the immigrant experience and the religious, social, political, economic and educational histories of a people.

My Generations is designed to guide the work of the student by the inclusion of instructional material and a liberal number of questions and exercises. The text together with this teacher's guide makes serious family history possible and practical.

Family history does not begin and end with a collection of names, dates, places and events. *My Generations* emphasizes that family history research is a *human quest*. While data are certainly valuable in themselves and necessary to motivate the researcher to continue his or her work, *how* people lived is equally, if not more, important to the family historian.

To trace one's family history back to the nineteenth, eighteenth, or seventeenth centuries is, of course, an exciting adventure, but unless one can also learn *how* people lived, the facts have no life to them. A family tree is bare without the leaves and flowers of song, story, legend, and yes, recipes of one's ancestors.

The logical order of subjects in *My Generations* highlights its effectiveness as a teaching tool in the classroom. The book begins with the child and those aspects of the child's life which are central: place in time and history; names; parents, siblings, grandparents and other relatives; nourishment; and the importance of the home as a gathering place for the family and keeper of family traditions and possessions. The book moves with the child to bar/bat mitzvah, to thinking about a career, and to marriage and maturity. *My Generations* clearly follows the life cycle.

As you walk through the book with your students, you will find that their worksheets will not all be filled at the same time. For example, your student may not be able to obtain her grandfather's signature (Chapter 3) until her next visit with him the following month. By then you may be reading Chapter 8 on marriage. There is some work that can only be done at an individual pace. Encourage this individual pacing. It emphasizes that the study of family history is ongoing and fluid and that one's success is in the pursuit of the goal as well as the goal itself. Keep up with your students' progress.

On those pages where students have to write a lot of information, suggest a planning sheet first. Where there is need for space for additional genealogical information, use duplicating master #6. In addition, you may suggest that your students attach a 7 ½ × 10 ½ envelope to the inside back cover of *My Generations* for the extra information and for miscellaneous papers.

The student who has limited access to family data must not be discouraged from engaging in this exciting and satisfying pursuit. If a student feels overwhelmed before he or she even begins, ask that student to sit with his mother or father and ask about times when either felt overwhelmed by a class in school. That student's quest as a family historian will have already begun at the kitchen table that night.

My Generations is a one-volume, self-contained reader and workbook. It asks the student to be actively engaged as a family historian. It cannot be emphasized enough that the student's success depends largely (at least at the start) on the teacher's own enthusiasm for the subject and the activities. *You should be a participant and not a spectator. Do the work along with your students*. Your own work as a family historian will encourage the work of your students. Good luck!

Lesson Plans

Lesson plans are built around each chapter. Each plan has six parts:

1. Aims of the Chapter
2. Jewish Values
3. Background
4. Glossary
5. Classroom Development
6. Suggested Classroom Activities

CHAPTER 1

WHERE ARE YOU?

Aims of the Chapter

To introduce the students to the concept of time. To introduce the process of migration (emigration and immigration): there are no special Jewish places—any place a Jew finds himself or herself is a Jewish place. To introduce the concept of personal history. To foster an understanding that knowledge of one's ancestors is knowledge of their way of life. To sketch how immigrants arrived in America. To assess the responsibility of the family historian.

Jewish Values

1. Responsibility for one's actions is a cornerstone of Jewish belief.
2. Each individual, though unique, is a member of the universal Jewish family.
3. Jewish history *is* family history. Jews are all part of one family.

Background

History

History rides on time; it travels along from one moment to the next. Each of us has been riding on time, moving along with history. While we are always in the process of creating our own personal history, we are part of the *universal* history of humankind *and* part of the *Jewish* history of mankind.

Nobody knows when history began, although many scientists and many religious traditions have speculated about it. Jewish tradition maintains that human history began when Adam and Eve were created by God. "And God created man in His image, in the image of God He created him; male and female He created them. God blessed them and God said to them, 'Be fertile and increase, fill the earth and master it; and rule the fish of the sea, the birds of the sky, and all the living things that creep on earth' " (Gen. 1:27–28).

According to the Torah, Adam and Eve began their history in the Garden of Eden. After they disobeyed God and ate the fruit of the Tree of Knowledge, they were banished from the Garden. It was the first time in history that people moved to a new home. From that point on, people have been moving all over the world. In *My Generations* Arthur Kurzweil writes: "One could say that history is, in part, the story of people and families moving from one place to another" (p. 7).

The Torah is replete with journeys people and families have taken: Noah, Abraham, Joseph, Moses, to name a few. Human history is the story of the journey from the beginning of history to the end of history. Right now we are somewhere in the middle.

Traditionally, Jews have long believed that history will end when the Messiah, *mashiakh,* comes. When the Messiah comes, there will be no more war and no more suffering. We cannot know when the end of history will come, but what we can do is to concern ourselves with living a good life—and this is our responsibility as Jews.

"Where Are You?"

After they ate the fruit of the Tree of Knowledge, "God called out to the man, and He said, 'Where are you?'" (Gen. 3:9). The first question that Adam and Eve had to answer when they entered human history was "Where are you?" In the same way, we begin our study of our history with this question: "Where are you—right now?"

The first question asked by *My Generations* actually echoes God's question to Adam: Where are you? As in the Torah itself, this course is designed to explore where we are—as Jews—on all levels: Where are we geographically? Where are we in Jewish history? Where are we in our families? Where are we in relation to a Jewish way of life? Where are we in relation to God?

The Jewish Immigrant to America

All Jews living in the United States of America today are immigrants or descendants of immigrants. People migrate for different reasons. Though Jews lived in America as early as 1654, large numbers of Jews did not arrive until the middle and latter half of the nineteenth century. They landed at the *Jewish* Plymouth Rock—Ellis Island in New York, and first settled in the *Jewish* Massachusetts Bay Colony—Manhattan's Lower East Side.

Ellis Island, a small Island in Upper New York Bay, was the major United States immigration station from 1892 to 1943. Today it is part of the Statue of Liberty National Monument, and since 1976 its dilapidated buildings have been open to the public. The National Parks Service, which maintains the Island, is presently working on its restoration.

Once a picnic site for early Dutch settlers, the Island was named for Samuel Ellis, its owner, in the latter part of the eighteenth century. Later purchased by the Federal government, it replaced Castle Garden at Manhattan's Battery Park as the major immigration station for European immigrants.

At its peak the station could process one million individuals a year. A total of twelve million people came through the Ellis Island station before settling on the mainland. It is estimated that two million of those were Jews. About one-third of the United States population today has ancestors who passed through the Island.

There were other ports of entry for Jews in America. Another major Jewish settlement was in Newport, Rhode Island. These Jewish settlers came from Portugal, Holland, South America, and the West Indies. Newport's Jewish community was the largest in America at the time of the American Revolution, and the Touro Synagogue in Newport is the oldest in the United States.

Charleston, South Carolina was a vibrant port city when Jewish travelers settled there in the eighteenth century, having emigrated from Western Europe and the West Indies. Boston, Baltimore, New Orleans, Philadelphia, and Galveston in the United States and Montreal, Quebec City, and Halifax in Canada were other ports of entry for Jewish immigrants.

Today, Jews can be found in every one of the fifty United States and in every one of the twelve provinces of Canada. More often than not, Jews live in large cities, among them: New York, Los Angeles, Chicago, Miami, Boston, and Philadelphia.

Jews have been city dwellers for many centuries. They were often not allowed to own land

and so they lived in towns and cities where they could own or rent houses. Also, Jews were restricted from working in certain trades. As merchants, traders, and manufacturers, Jews depended heavily upon centers of population.

Judaism is a community way of life. For example, Jews require ten adults to form a minyan for prayer. This tradition encourages Jews to be a communal people. If they lived too far from one another, it would have been difficult, if not impossible, to join together for prayer services. Jews celebrate together, pray together, mourn together, and generally live close to each other.

Learning about Jewish history will help us to understand our own personal history. Learning about both at the same time will help us to gain insight into each other and reveal how interrelated we are. We begin with ourselves, our immediate family, and the neighborhood in which we live.

Glossary

1. *Ancestor*—a person from whom others are descended
2. *Emigration*—the movement *from* a country, region, or place of habitation to settle in another
   emigrate—to move from a country, region, or place of habitation to settle in another
   emigrant—a person who emigrates
3. *Immigration*—the movement *to* a country, region, or place of habitation of which one is not native
   immigrate—to move *to* a country, region, or place of habitation of which one is not native
   immigrant—a person who immigrates
4. *Genealogy*—the study of family ancestries and histories
5. *Migration*—the movement *from* one country, region, or place of habitation to settle in another
   migrate—to move from one country, region, or place of habitation to settle in another
   migrant—a person who migrates
6. *Ship's manifest*—a list of passengers

Finding and Pronouncing Geographic Locations

Students will hear the names of the places where their families are from and will not always know how to spell them, find them on a map, or even pronounce them. One of the towns featured in *My Generations* is a good example. The Kurzweil family pronounces their ancestral town "pshem-ish." It is spelled PRZEMYSL.

There are, however, library sources that will be helpful; among them are the following:

The Columbia Lippincott Gazetteer of the World with 1961 Supplement. Edited by Leon E. Seltzer. 1952. New York: Columbia University Press.

The Macmillan World Gazetteer and Geographical Dictionary. Edited by T. C. Collocott and J. O. Thorne. 1955. New York: Macmillan Pub. Co.

Place Name Changes Since 1900: A World Gazetteer. Compiled by Adrian Room. 1979. Metuchen, New Jersey: The Scarecrow Press.

Webster's New Geographical Dictionary. 1972. Springfield, Massachusetts: G. & C. Merriam Co.

The world of maps is a fascinating one. Perhaps a local librarian familiar with maps, gazetteers, and geographic sources could give a presentation to your class.

Classroom Development

Brainstorming, a popular and effective teaching tool, can be successful in motivating students to think about themselves and their families.

Write the words "a *parent* is" on the board and and ask students to give brief definitions.

Write the definitions as the students call them out (or have a student act as secretary). Do this also with the following: "a *child* is"; "a *grandparent* is"; "a *neighborhood* is."

After the board is filled, point to a definition such as: "A *parent* is a friend" and ask your students a question such as: "When was your parent a friend to you?" or "When did you *need* your parent to be a friend to you?" Point to another definition such as: "A *neighborhood* is a place where I can be myself" and ask the students a question such as: "Where do you go in your neighborhood to be yourself?" or "Where is your favorite place in your neighborhood?"

A short writing experience could follow:

1. "My neighborhood and why you should visit it."
2. "My oldest living relative and the times we have spent together."
3. "A story my (grandfather, grandmother, etc.) (told, tells) me."
4. "A family reunion."
5. "The relative I never knew."
6. "A letter to a relative I don't see any more."

Role playing is another effective teaching tool. It can be successful in helping students define the concepts of migration, emigration, immigration, and resettlement.

Here are several situations in which the student can gain insight into these concepts.

1. An immigrant Jewish family crossing the ocean.
2. An immigrant Jewish family arriving at Ellis Island.
3. An immigrant Jewish child in conflict with immigrant parents.
4. An *American-born* Jewish child in conflict with immigrant parents.
5. A Jewish immigrant child attending public school for the first time.
6. A recent Jewish immigrant (perhaps a Russian Jew) being interviewed.

Allow your students time before engaging in the role playing to think about the situation and about the roles they will play. They may want to ask *you* how *they* should play the roles and what *their* goals should be. While they may need some background information, it would be best to allow them their own insights.

The role playing is best confined to a five-minute period so the situations are quickly defined and the students don't lose interest. Don't stop the children during their performances even if you think they are moving out of the situation. Remember, *you* don't know what their goals are.

Have two children act as reporters to write a brief news story of the event. Allow the performers to react first to their own performances and then have the reporters and the rest of the class react.

A short writing experience could follow:

1. "There's no place like home."
2. "The United States (your city) is/is not the place to spend the rest of my life."
3. "Travel broadens one's horizons."
4. "Travel is a fool's paradise."
5. "Why we moved."
6. "When (name of relative or friend) moved away from me."

The short essays can be read in class. They can later be displayed on the class bulletin board and/or included in the class newspaper or magazine. (See "Suggested Classroom and Homework Activities.")

Suggested Classroom and Homework Activities

The bulletin board is an important place in any classroom and each classroom should have its own board. All completed class and homework assignments suggested throughout this guide may be displayed. The materials on the board should be changed periodically to keep the students interested in them. The board should be designed and maintained by the students themselves.

Another project for students is writing and printing a newspaper or magazine that would include appropriate completed writing and drawing assignments reflecting family history research. (Remember: photographs can be successfully photocopied without damaging them.)

1. On page 9 in *My Generations,* there is space for students to draw a map of their neighborhood. Encourage your students to take a walking tour of their neighborhood to sketch their map before writing in the book. See duplicating master #1.
2. Ask students to pretend to be grandparents and to write letters to imaginary grandchildren describing their neighborhood.
3. Ask students to ask their parents for the name and address of a relative they have never met and to write to that relative. Students should introduce themselves and state the purpose of their letter before asking any questions. Questions should be short and only a few should be written to increase chances of a response. Here are some questions that might be asked: 1) Were you born in Europe? Where? If not, who were the immigrants in your family who came to America? Where did they come from? 2) What were your parents' names? Your mother's maiden name? 3) What are the names and ages of the people in your family (brothers, sisters, children) and where do they live?

   Your students should enclose a self-addressed stamped envelope for the respondent's convenience. (For letters outside the United States, include a self-addressed envelope and an International Reply Coupon available at your post office.)
4. Genealogy, like stamp collecting, can become a lifelong hobby. Duplicating master #2 can be used to introduce genealogical research to your students.

   There are a few dozen Jewish historical societies and Jewish genealogical societies in the United States alone, reflecting a growing interest in our subject. You might want to invite a guest to your classroom who can show your students the kinds of material they may find when they become genealogists.

   At the same time, you can expose your students to the growing literature on the subject of Jewish genealogy. The author of *My Generations,* Arthur Kurzweil, has written *From Generation to Generation: How to Trace Your Jewish Genealogy and Personal History,* a guidebook for Jewish genealogists. There are other books on the subject as well. (See the "Genealogist's Bookshelf" on page 51.)
5. We have already noted the following quotation from *My Generations:* "One could say that history is, in part, the story of people and families moving from one place to another." Using duplicating master #3, see how familiar your students are with some of the more famous "moves" of Jewish history.

Here is the answer key for the fill-in-the-blank exercise:

1. The Garden of Eden
2. Haran
3. Egypt
4. Babylonia
5. Spain
6. New Amsterdam
7. German
8. Russia
9. Germany
10. Israel

Chapter 1 at a glance:

Activities in My Generations:

1. My Neighborhood (p. 9)

2. My Community (pp. 12–13)
3. Family Residence Record (pp. 14–16)
4. Where I Have Lived (p. 17)
5. My Immigrant Ancestors (pp. 20–21)
6. Photographs of My Immigrant Ancestors (pp. 24–25)

Duplicating Masters:

1. A Map Of My Neighboorhood (#1)
2. Guide To Sources For Further Research (#2)
3. Famous Jewish Moves And Mine (#3)

CHAPTER 2

WHERE DO YOU COME FROM?

Aims of the Chapter

To view Judaism as an inheritance. To introduce the nature of heredity. To identify the uniqueness of each family and of each family's personal history. To note that throughout history, Jews have spoken many languages and that language is a reflection of uniqueness. To describe ancestral charts.

Jewish Values

1. Jews are the inheritors of their religious tradition. As humans, we inherit physical characteristics from our forbears. As Jews we inherit Judaism. As the kiddush says, "Praised be Thou, Lord our God, who has hallowed us with Thy commandments, and has favored us with the gracious gift of the Sabbath as our loving inheritance."
2. Family consciousness, fostered by a child's obligation to honor his or her parents, has been a value since tribal times. By recording events in ancestors' lives and preserving family documents and photographs, the student honors his or her family and its history.
3. While Jews cherish their uniqueness, they respect, value, and welcome the various lifestyles of Jews in their own community and in Jewish communities around the world.
4. Jews are sensitive to strangers because throughout their history, they have been *strangers in strange lands*: "You too must befriend the stranger, for you were strangers in the land of Egypt" (Deut. 10:19).

Background

Heredity

No more than an elementary knowledge of heredity is necessary to understand this chapter. Heredity is the property in all living organisms that ensures that the biological qualities of parents reappear in their offspring. Hereditary transmission is the passage from ancestors to descendants of an organized collection of elementary living units, known as genes, that condition the organism's response to its environment.

Familial Responsibility

Among Jews there has always been a high moral standard for conducting family life. Jews have also always shown concern for the welfare of the needy, the homeless, and orphans. The vast number of Jewish social service organizations reflect this fact. One might say, then, that Jews have always lived according to the notion of the *extended* family.

When God asked Cain, "Where is your brother Abel?" He was establishing the standard for Jewish family life: responsibility for one another. After Cain answered, "I do not know/Am I my brother's keeper?" the disappointed God commanded that Abel be "a ceaseless wanderer on earth," with no one to be responsible for him (Gen. 1:9–12).

The Tower of Babel

With respect to language, the Tower of Babel story is insightful. This story in Genesis (11:1–26) attempts to explain the origin of the variety of world languages *and* the reason the human population dispersed and populated the world.

> All the earth had the same language and the same words. And as men migrated from the east, they came upon a valley in the land of Shinar and settled there. They said to one another, "Come, let us make bricks and burn them hard." Brick served them as stone, and bitumen served them as mortar. And they said, "Come, let us build us a city, and a tower with its top in the sky, to make a name for ourselves; else we shall be scattered all over the world." The Lord came down to look at the city and tower which man had built, and the Lord said, "If, as one people with one language for all, this is how they have begun to act, then nothing that they may propose to do will be out of reach. Let us, then, go down and confound their speech there, so that they shall not understand one another's speech." Thus the Lord scattered them from there over the face of the whole earth; and they stopped building the city. That is why it was called Babel, because there the Lord confounded the speech of the whole earth; and from there the Lord scattered them over the face of the whole earth.

What If A Student Is Adopted?

The teacher must understand the special needs of the adopted child and his or her adoptive *and* natural parents. There are organizations which can help someone search for his or her natural parents. As the teacher, you will have to decide in each individual case how much information you want to reveal to your students. Certainly before *you* give *any* information to the students, conversations with the rabbi and the children's adoptive parents should be held.

What you need to emphasize is that children who are adopted may adopt the ancestry of their adoptive family. After all, the family adopted them and therefore they are invited to share their adoptive family's history. Such a process is not unique. When two adults marry, the husband and wife each adopt the family of the other, *including its history*.

Each new American "adopts" the history of this country. While your family was probably not on this continent when the Declaration of Independence was signed, the 4th of July is a holiday we celebrate: we adopt American history as our own. Similarly, an adopted child adopts the history of his or her new family.

For those children who do want to pursue a search for their natural parents, the Adoptees' Liberty Movement Association (ALMA) can help. Write to:

ALMA P.O. Box 154 Washington Bridge Station New York, New York 10003	ALMA P.O. Box 112 Lomita, California 90717

Books by Betty Jean Lifton (see "Genealogist's Bookshelf," p. 51) and Florence Fisher will be helpful.

Glossary

1. *Aramaic*—the everyday language of the Jews of Babylonia

2. *Brit Milah*—the covenant of circumcision
3. *Judezmo*—the traditional Jewish language of Sephardic Jews.

Classroom Development

Whom do I see when I see me? This exercise can help students focus on themselves with respect to their physical and personal characteristics; in addition, this activity can help them see themselves as both *branch* and *trunk* in the *family forest*.

Write about the following topics on the board and give the students time to think about each, to select one, and to jot down some responses that you will later ask them to share with the class.

After each student has had an opportunity to talk about his or her responses, assign a short writing exercise allowing each student to choose a topic from the ones listed on the board. The essays can be read in class and later displayed on the class bulletin board and/or included in the class newspaper or magazine.

1. "The values I hold dear."
2. "Being the (youngest, oldest, middle, only) child in my family has made the difference in who I am today."
3. "Our vanishing species—me!"
4. "People don't see me as I really am."
5. "When I look in the mirror, this is who I see."
6. "If you want to know me, you have to know the family I love, the friends I have, the books I read, etc."
7. "Being myself."
8. "The (aunt, uncle, cousin) I admire."
9. "I am ____________."
10. "I am not ____________."
11. "I can always be called upon to ____________."

Suggested Classroom and Homework Activities

1. Ask students to imagine what it would have been like for their ancestors crossing the Atlantic Ocean by steamship. Have them write a narrative dramatizing the experience.

2. Visit places of importance for Jewish immigrants in America. In New York City, the places to visit include: the Lower East Side, Williamsburg, Boro Park, the Jewish Museum, the Israeli Consulate, Ellis Island, the Statue of Liberty. (Consult the Bernard Postal books for places to visit outside New York City.

   Of course, you need not go too far to find places of importance for Jewish immigrants in America. Start in your own community. Ask your students to identify the oldest house, school, synagogue, business, neighborhood. Your local library will have information and so will the oldest resident in your community or congregation. (In this regard, you may want to take the class on a visit to a senior citizen's home.)

Relationship Chart (See Master #4)

3. How many times have you had conversations with relatives of yours when you tried to figure out how you were related? There is often confusion regarding the names of the relationships between people. For example, do you know the difference between a second cousin and a first cousin once removed? What does "once removed" mean? Is it possible for you to be your own cousin? The following chart will clear up any confusion you might have with the definitions of relationships. This is an easy system for you to use to answer the question: How are we related?

   First we need to define some terms.

   Common Progenitor. The closest ancestor which two people have in common is their common progenitor. So, for example, you and your sister have your parents as your common progenitors. You also have your grandparents and great-grandparents in common, but for the purpose of this chart we are only concerned with your *closest* common ancestor. To give another example, the common progenitor of you and your first cousin is one of your grandparents. In other words, you and your first cousin do not have the same parents, but you do have the same grandparents.

Removed. When we speak of a cousin being once removed, we are referring to generations. For example, if you know who your father's first cousin is, then you are that person's first cousin once removed. That is, you are one generation away (or removed) from that person. Subsequently, if you know your grandfather's first cousin, then you are that person's first cousin twice removed. You are two generations from that person.

Cousin. A cousin is a child of your aunts and uncles, great-aunts and great-uncles, and so on.

With those terms understood, you will now be able to understand and determine your relationships with your relatives.

As you see on the chart on duplicating master #4, there are numbers from 0 to 6 across the top and down the left side. These numbers represent the number of generations from a common progenitor. The square in the upper left corner which says "CP" stands for common progenitor.

The first thing you must do is to figure out who the common progenitor between two people is. For example, suppose that you want to know the relationship between yourself and your first cousin's son. The first question to ask is: Who is the closest ancestor to both of us? The answer is your grandfather (or grandmother, but for simplicity, the chart shows only male descent though it is the same for males and females).

On the left-hand column, notice that the square next to number 2 says GS, which stands for grandson. That is *you* (in our example). On the row across the top, you can see that the square below number 3 says GGS, which means great-grandson. That is your first cousin's son. Again, your grandfather and your first cousin's son's great-grandfather are the same person. On the chart, you are number 2 and he is number 3.

The square at which row 2 and 3 meet tells you the relationship. That is, the square which says "ICIR" is the square where row 2 and row 3 meet. ICIR means "first cousin once removed." That is your relationship to each other.

By the way, "once removed" works both ways. You are his first cousin once removed and he is your first cousin once removed.

Try the chart with a few examples from your family to get used to determining relationships.

Finally, to the question, "Can you be your own cousin?" the answer is yes. If, for example, your great-grandparents were first cousins when they married, then you are your own fourth cousin!

4. Many people see the link between family history and Jewish genetic diseases. There are diseases which Jews are more prone to than any other ethnic group. Students who may want to report on the subject can write for information to:

   National Foundation for Jewish Genetic Diseases, Inc.
   609 Fifth Avenue
   New York, New York 10017

5. Yiddish was the language of everyday life in the shtetl. It uses the Hebrew alphabet but evolved out of the German language heard by Jewish settlers in northern France about 1000 years ago. As Jews settled throughout Germany, they added words from other languages. Yiddish is three-fourths German and one-fourth Hebrew, Polish, Russian, and Rumanian. Many Yiddish-words have entered the English vocabulary. Your students may have someone in their family who still speaks the language. Invite that person to talk to the class. See duplicating master #5.

6. In recent years, there has been an increase in the immigrant Russian Jewish population. In fact, so many Russian Jews have settled in the Brighton Beach community of Brooklyn, New York that the area has been nicknamed, "Odessa by the Sea." Are there recent Russian immigrants in your community or Jewish immigrants from other Eastern European countries, Israel, or South America? Your students may be their classmates in public school or in other religious school classes. Invite several to your class to talk about their journey to America.

7. The world Jewish population is considered to be *native* to three areas: *Ashkenazim* are Jews from Eastern and Central Europe; *Sephardim* are Jews originally from Spain and Portugal, and *Oriental Jews* are from North Africa, the Middle East, Iran, India, and other Asian countries. Those students interested in learning more about Jews around the world may want to report on:

   a) the Golden age of Spanish Jewry 900–1200 C.E.
   b) Marranos
   c) Ethiopian Jewry
   d) Famous Sephardim such as Judah ha-Levi, Maimonides, Joseph Caro, Benjamin Cardozo
   e) the Jews of Argentina
   f) the Jews of Iran
   g) the Jews of South Africa

8. In *My Generations* Arthur Kurzweil writes "Use the book as a tool, keeping in mind that you and your family are unique!" (p. 26). Because each family *is* different, your students may find the space provided in the book inadequate to record their genealogical data. Duplicating master #6 will provide your students with extra pages for added material.

Chapter 2 at a glance:

Activities in My Generations:

1. Birth Registration Certificate (p. 27)
2. Brit Milah Certificate (p. 28)
3. Certificate for Naming a Child (p. 29)
4. My Father's Genealogy (pp. 30–31)
5. My Mother's Genealogy (pp. 32–33)
6. Genealogical Data (pp. 34–35)
7. My Family Tree (pp. 38–39)
8. My Family Look-alikes (p. 41)
9. Languages in My Family (p. 42)

Duplicating Masters:

1. How Are We Related (#4)
2. Yiddish Is More Than A Language (#5)
3. Additional Genealogical Data (#6)

CHAPTER 3

WHAT IS YOUR NAME?

Aims of the Chapter

To learn the importance Jews place on naming and to learn about the ceremonies and traditions of naming. To discover for whom we are named (our namesake) and why. To understand that a name gets its real value from what the person who bears it does with his or her life. To learn that Jewish surnames have specific meanings in their origins.

Jewish Values

1. The value of a name depends on the actions of the person whose name it is. Rabbi Simeon said: "There are three crowns: being a priest, being a king, being a scholar of the Torah. But the crown of a good name is greater than all three."
2. The value of *zachor*—remembrance—is evident in Jewish naming customs.

Background

Naming and Re-naming

Naming things and people is an important part of Jewish tradition. The Torah tells us that after God created Adam and Eve, he gave them their names. After creating the animals, God instructed Adam to give *them* their names.

Jews are called Semites because we are descendants of one of Noah's three sons, Shem. Shem is our direct ancestor. Shem means *name*. We come from the son named *name*. There is an additional point of interest with the name Shem. We call God *Hashem*, which means *the name*. So, we descend from *name* and we call God who created us *the name*. It should be clear by now that names are important in Jewish tradition.

Re-naming for various reasons has also been part of Jewish tradition. Later in Genesis, we learn that Abraham was originally called Abram and Sarah was called Sarai. It is a dramatic moment in the Torah when God re-names them both. (Gen. 17:5 and 17:15). Their changed names reflect their changed fates. Suddenly, Abraham and Sarah become the father and mother of the Jewish people.

Stories are told about how many Jews, when they arrived in America, had their last names changed by immigration officials who could not spell long, unusual-sounding Jewish names. But many Jews changed their own names. *Rosenberg* was changed to *Rose, Cohen* to *Kane*, and so on. At times, the reason for this was to make the name sound *less Jewish*. Due to anti-Semitism, many Jews were only able to obtain employment by withholding information about their Jewish backgrounds. In fact, many Jews did achieve success in this manner and their fate was changed.

The late Golda Meir was a Prime Minister of Israel. Her given name was Golda Myerson. David Ben-Gurion, Israel's first Prime Minister, was given the name David Gruen at birth. In these cases, names were changed to celebrate being Jewish.

Another common practice of name-changing in Jewish tradition occurs when someone is very ill. Many Jews believed that if you changed an ill person's name, then the Angel of Death would become confused and would not be able to find the person.

Surnames

Jews did not always have last names. Last names were not necessary when Jews lived in small towns and had little contact with the outside world. Someone could have been called Chaim ben Moshe all his life, never needing a last name. Or he could have been called Chaim the Baker, based on his profession as a baker. That, too, would have been enough.

However, about 200 years ago, European countries began requiring Jews to take last names and to officially register them. This fact does not necessarily mean that your name did not exist in your family 200 years ago. It might have. But when the laws regarding Jews registering names appeared, Jews had to either keep the last names they had, or choose new last names, or be given a last name by the government officials.

In 1787, in the Austrian Empire (which today includes much of Austria, Poland, Hungary, and parts of Russia) Jews had to choose last names and register them. The same was true in Russia in 1834 and in Napoleon's empire in 1808. Before these dates, Jews could change last names when they wanted to, or could go without them.

The Jewish communities reacted to these laws in a variety of ways. Some Jewish communities asked the rabbi of the town to assign last names. Other communities were assigned last names by the government officials in the town. But others were able to choose their own names.

Sephardic Naming Practices

Many Sephardic Jews adopted surnames from the Arabs who used a patronymic ("ibn") to designate "son of" but would also often add the father's name without the use of "ibn." Occupational names, nicknames, and place names were also popular among the Arabs. For example, Abulafia means "father of medicine," and Gabbai means "synagogue official." Among place names taken as surnames are Cardozo (Spain) and Montefiore (Italy).

Finally, it is well known that while Ashkenazic Jews will not name a child after a person who is still living, Sephardic Jews will.

Glossary

1. *Ashkenazi*—a Jew of central or Eastern Europe and descendants
2. *Matronymic*—name derived from mother's name or maternal ancestor
3. *Patronymic*—name derived from father's name or paternal ancestor
4. *Sephardi*—a Jew of Spain, Portugal, or the Middle East, including North Africa and descendants

Classroom Development

Benzion Kaganoff's book, *A Dictionary of Jewish Names and their History*, would be helpful here.

Write the name of each student on a separate piece of paper. Before class select several pieces of paper at random and place these between the pages of the Kaganoff book. Tell your students, "I have each of your names written on a piece of paper. I'm going to *give* you your names. Hold them carefully. We'll use them in a later exercise."

Distribute all but the name slips in the book. To those students say, "I'm sorry; I don't have names for you. I must have misplaced them. I'll look for them later." The students whose name slips are "lost" will be uncomfortable. Those to whom you have "given" names will probably sit quietly and firmly clasp the name slips in their hands. You will have begun to impress upon your students the importance of names.

After each child has been "given" his or her name (except for those whose name slips are "lost") write the words "a *name* is" or "my *name* means" on the board and ask students to give brief definitions. Write the definitions as the students call them out (or have a student act as secretary). Do this also with the following: "my (mother's, father's) name is"; "I was named after . . ."; "if I could choose my own name, it would be. . ."

After the board is filled, point to a definition such as, "I was named after my grandfather," and ask your students a question such as, "Why did your parents choose your grandfather's name for you?" or "Did you ever meet your grandfather? What did you like best about him?"

A short writing experience could follow:

1. "The person after whom I was named."
2. "Why my grandfather changed the family name."
3. "Why I would change my name."
4. "Why I would never change my name."

The short essays could be read in class. They could later be developed into longer pieces, displayed on the class bulletin board, and/or included in the class newspaper or magazine.

Return to the Kaganoff book. Select one student at random and tell him or her you will look up his or her name in the section in the book on names. As you turn the pages, you will "accidentally" come across the name slips you "misplaced." Gather them quickly. "I have found your names." You have identified the contemporary concern with the importance of names and the Jew's obligation to remember them and to honor them.

Suggested Classroom and Homework Activities

1. One practice of name-changing in Jewish tradition has to do with changing one's fate. When someone is very ill, a name-changing ritual, *Shinui Ha-Shem*, is performed in the synagogue. The Torah is opened at random. The critically ill person is given the first name that is read. (Remember, it is believed that if you change the name of the ill person, you confuse the Angel of Death.) Ask each student if there is a story like this one in his or her family.

2. It is interesting to study the cycle of names. Have each student begin with people his or her own age. List the first English names of ten people. Then list the first names of their mother and father. Afterwards, list the names of their grandparents, if they know these names. (This exercise could be confined to the classroom alone and each student could list the names in his or her family.) For example, why would *Mendel* name his son *Morris* and *Morris* name his son *Maurice* and *Maurice* name his son *Mark*?

3. Ask each student to look for his or her surname in the *Encyclopedia Judaica* (family name or maternal family name) and write a report on the history of the name, and of famous people who have had the same name. Your students may also want to find out what their

4. Have your students prepare oral reports on the celebration of a *pidyon ha-ben*, redemption of the firstborn. You may want them to read the story of Jacob and Esau (Gen. 25:19–34); the priestly service of the firstborn (Num. 3:1–4:49), and the story of the redemption of the firstborn (Num. 18:15–18).

5. The importance of names in Jewish tradition is reflected in the prominence names are given in the Torah. See duplicating master #7 for an activity to help your students focus on names in the Torah.
6. Many Jews have changed their names to make them sound "less Jewish." How familiar are your students with Jewish entertainers who have changed their names? See duplicating master #8.

   Here are the answers:

1–D	8–K	15–V	22–Q
2–I	9–G	16–W	23–P
3–A	10–L	17–T	24–U
4–B	11–N	18–S	25–O
5–C	12–F	19–R	26–Z
6–J	13–M	20–X	
7–H	14–E	21–Y	

7. People's signatures are as distinct as their names and often reveal aspects of their personality. On page 48 in *My Generations*, your students are asked to record family signatures. Duplicating master #9 introduces students to the signatures of famous people. Here is some background information about these individuals.

   Stephen S. Wise (1874–1949) was founder of New York City's Free Synagogue (1907) and the American Jewish Congress (1916) and the foremost spokesman for Reform Judaism during the first half of the twentieth century.

   Sholem Aleichem (1859–1916) was an Eastern European Yiddish writer of shtetl life whose stories were turned into the musical *Fiddler on the Roof*.

   Theodor Herzl (1860–1904) was an early Zionist who in 1897 in Basel, Switzerland convened the First Zionist Congress, which launched the political movement to create a Jewish state.

   Sigmund Freud (1856–1939) was an Austrian-born physician who founded psychoanalysis.

   Maimonides (1135–1204) was Rabbi Moses ben Maimon or Rambam, a great scholar, philosopher, and physician of the Golden Age of Spanish Jewry.

   Albert Einstein (1879–1955) was an escapee from Nazi Germany who became the greatest scientist of the twentieth century.

   Benjamin Disraeli (1804–1881) was a British statesman who was Prime Minister of Great Britain when Victoria was Queen.

   Louis D. Brandeis (1856–1941) was the first Jewish United States Supreme Court Justice. (He served from 1916–1939.) Brandeis University in Massachusetts is named after him.

   David Ben-Gurion (1886–1973) was Israel's first Prime Minister and the man who delivered to the world Israel's Proclamation of Independence on May 14, 1948.

Chapter 3 at a glance:

Activities in My Generations:

1. My Names (p. 45)
2. My Namesake (p. 46)
3. My Relatives' Namesakes (p. 47)
4. Family Signatures (p. 48)

Duplicating Masters:

1. Names In The Torah (#7)
2. Famous Jews Who Have Changed Their Names (#8)
3. Famous Signatures (#9)
4. What's In A Name? More Than You Think (#10)

CHAPTER 4

WHAT DO YOU EAT?

Aims of the Chapter

To learn that recipes passed from generation to generation are part of our family history. To learn that the special food customs associated with our holidays connect generations and are a part of our Jewish history. To stress the cultural uniqueness of the kosher laws—the laws of kashrut. To learn that Jews contribute to other cultures and absorb from other cultures.

Jewish Values

1. Special foods make special times *special* and help to characterize our cultural inheritance.
2. Any activity, including cooking and baking, which supports the cultural uniqueness of Jewish living is to be encouraged.

Background

Food in the Bible

The first reference to food in the Bible is in Genesis: "And God said, 'Let the earth sprout vegetation: seed-bearing plants, fruit trees of every kind on earth that bear fruit with the seed in it.' And it was so. The earth brought forth vegetation: seed-bearing plants of every kind, and trees of every kind bearing fruit with the seed in it. And God saw that this was good. And there was evening and there was morning, a third day" (Gen. 1:11–13). God then created living creatures, including the human.

Afterwards, Genesis reads: "God said, 'See, I give you every seed-bearing plant that is upon all the earth, and every tree that has seed-bearing fruit; they shall be yours for food. And to all the animals on land, to all the birds of the sky and to everything that creeps on earth in which there is the breath of life [I give] all the green plants for food.' And it was so. And God saw all that He had made and found it very good. And there was evening and there was morning, the sixth day." (It may be interesting to note here that according to the Bible, humans and other creatures became carnivorous only *after* the Flood.) To Noah, God said: "Every creature that lives shall be yours to eat; as with the green grasses, I give you all these" (Gen. 9:3). Maybe God's permission to eat flesh was His way of recognizing human vulnerability to evil. According to Isaiah, when the Messiah comes, humans and other living beings will once again become vegetarians.)

The wolf shall dwell with the lamb,
The leopard lie down with the kid;

The calf, the beast of prey, and the fatling together,
With a little boy to lead them.
The cow and the bear shall graze,
Their young shall lie down together;
And the lion, like the ox, shall eat straw.
A babe shall play
Over a viper's hole.
And an infant pass his hand
Over an adder's den.
In all my sacred Mount
Nothing evil or vile shall be done;
For the land shall be filled with devotion to the Lord
As waters cover the sea.

(Isaiah 11:6–9)

Kashrut

Kashrut is the term applied to the dietary laws as specified in the Torah (Leviticus 11:44–45, Deuteronomy 14:21, and Exodus 22:30) and a *kosher home* is one in which these laws are carefully attended to. When a Jew "keeps" kosher, it is thought that he or she is set apart from the world and is connected to prior generations. The Jew becomes holy through adherence to these laws. Among the foods a Jew is permitted are all vegetables and plants; the meat of all four-footed animals which chew the cud *and* have parted hoofs; all fish having *both* fins and scales, and all fowl (known by tradition to be kosher). Among the prohibitions are all insects and reptiles, blood, and any mixture of meat and milk.

Classroom Development

Still another effective teaching tool to motivate students to think about the subject for your lesson is *word association*. This tool can be successful here in helping students think about food customs. Unlike brainstorming, word association calls for rapid-fire responses of one, two, or, at most, three words. Write the responses on the board as the students call them out (or, again have a student act as secretary).

Instead of asking for volunteers, work around the room calling for a response to each word from each student. This activity could also be called the "fast *food* chain."

Ask for responses to the following:

appetizer	bagel	lox	kugel
chicken soup	matzah	Shabbat dinner	herring
kosher	blintzes	motzi	delicatessen
chopped liver	bialy	kiddish	Passover
Purim	Succot	horse raddish	matzah brie

A short writing experience could follow:

1. "My favorite meal is . . ."
2. "When I have dinner with my (grandparent, aunt, uncle, any relative) . . ."
3. "I like to eat because . . ."
4. "I love to help my mother cook/bake . . ."
5. "When my father is in the kitchen . . ."

The short essays can be read in class. They can later be displayed on the class bulletin board and/or included in the class newspaper or magazine.

Suggested Classroom and Homework Activities

1. There is space in Chapter 4 in *My Generations* for your students to write four special family recipes. Ask each student to cook or bake at home one of these recipes and rewrite the

recipe on the form provided by duplicating master #11. Set aside at least two class meetings during which time each student will talk about the tradition of that food in the family and allow other students to sample the food. The recipes may be collected in a book with copies distributed to each student. Drawings may accompany the text.

2. Everyone has a favorite holiday food. Duplicating master #12 gives your students a chance to match favorite holiday foods with the holiday during which they are enjoyed.

3. *Chicken soup* has a reputation for being the "ultimate" cure-all and transcends religion, race, and national origin. Even Dr. Barney Clark, the first person to receive an artificial heart, was given chicken soup as his first meal after his operation. Ask each student to tell a favorite chicken soup story.

4. Food as *symbol* is introduced early in Jewish tradition.

   Now the serpent was the shrewdest of all the wild beasts that the Lord God had made. He said to the woman, "Did God really say: You shall not eat of any tree of the garden?" The woman replied to the serpent, "We may eat of the fruit of the other trees of the garden. It is only about fruit of the tree in the middle of the garden that God said: "You shall not eat of it or touch it, lest you die." And the serpent said to the woman, "You are not going to die, but God knows that as soon as you eat of it your eyes will be opened and you will be like divine beings who know good and bad." When the woman saw that the tree was good for eating and a delight to the eyes, and that the tree was desirable as a source of wisdom, she took of its fruit and ate. She also gave some to her husband, and he ate. Then the eyes of both of them were opened and they perceived that they were naked; and they sewed together fig leaves and made themselves loincloths.
   (Gen. 2:1–7)

   Ask each student to tell a food as *symbol* story.

5. In His instructions to Noah, God said, in part: "And of all that lives, of all flesh, you shall take two of each into the ark and keep alive with you; they shall be male and female. From birds of every kind, cattle of every kind, every kind of creeping thing on earth, two of each shall come to you to stay alive. For your part, take of everything that is eaten and store it away, to serve as food for you and for them." (Gen. 6:19–21)

   Have each student read commentary on these instructions and answer the following question: What did Noah, his family, and the animals eat for forty days? Each student should prepare a brief report for presentation to the class.

6. Ask each student: What is your level of kashrut observance? Do you follow any of the laws of kashrut? Are you strict about them? Is there a difference between what you eat at home and what you eat outside of your home? Ask each student to explain his or her level of kashrut observance.

   Remind your students that each generation of Jews responds in its own way to the laws of kashrut. There is more than one way to be Jewish, even when it comes to keeping kosher.

Chapter 4 at a glance:

Activities in My Generations:

1. Favorite Holiday Foods (p. 51)
2. Family Recipe (p. 53)
3. Family Recipe (p. 55)
4. Family Recipe (p. 56)
5. Family Recipe (p. 58)

Duplicating Masters:

1. A Special Family Recipe (#11)
2. Favorite Holiday Foods (#12)

CHAPTER 5

YOUR MOST IMPORTANT POSSESSIONS

Aims of the Chapter

To stress that Jewish tradition is rich with *things* to help make Jewish life more meaningful and rewarding. To show that many of our holidays and customs require ritual objects and that these objects are often kept in the family from generation to generation. To portray books and photographs as among the oldest possessions in a household. To demonstrate that like our parents and grandparents, we will have experiences, sights, and objects *new* in our lifetime that we will want to pass on to our children.

Jewish Values

1. Ritual objects connect us to the customs and traditions of our family and to our Jewish heritage.
2. Jews don't *make* things into idols; we *use* things to connect us to our people and our tradition.

Background

Ritual Objects

> R. Levi said: The rod that was created at twilight on the eve of the Sabbath was given to Adam in the Garden of Eden. Adam turned it over to Enoch, Enoch turned it over to Noah, Noah turned it over to Shem, Shem turned it over to Abraham, Abraham turned it over to Isaac, Isaac to Jacob. Jacob brought it to Egypt and turned it over to his son Joseph. When Joseph died, his entire property, including the rod, was confiscated and taken to Pharoh's palace. Now Jethro was one of the magicians of Egypt, and when he saw the rod, he read the signs upon it and put forth his hand and took it. Then when Moses came to Jethro's house he too saw the rod and read the signs on it. When Jethro saw him he said: This is he who will deliver Israel from Egypt. Therefore he gave his daughter to Moses for a wife. With the aid of the rod, Moses kept Jethro's sheep for 40 years. . . . .
>
> (Tanna Debe Eliyyahu S.54)

Jewish tradition provides us with many ritual objects: kiddish cups, kippot, teffillin, tzitzit, mezuzot, Shabbat candlesticks. Many of our holidays have ritual objects associated specifically with them. On Succot, we have etrogim and lulavim; on Pesach, we have seder plates, matzah covers, and a special cup for Elijah.

The Torah

The greatest Jewish object is the Torah and there are many ritual objects associated with it. Its home is an *aron ha-kodesh*, the ark, in front of which is the *parochet*, or curtain. Above the ark, a *ner tamid*, an eternal light burns continuously.

Within the ark, the Torah sits. It is wrapped around two staves, *azei hayyim*, trees of life. On the top of the two trees of life are beautiful decorations of silver or gold called *rimmonim*. Often, the Torah will have a larger crown called a *keter Torah*.

The Torah is also wrapped with a soft mantle, almost always decorated. On top of the mantle a silver breastplate rests, a rememberance of the breastplate worn by the high priest in Temple times.

Traditionally, the parchment of a Torah must not be touched and so it is read with the aid of a *yad*, a hand. When it is read, it is placed on a *mappah*, a desk covering which is usually an embroidered cloth which serves as a cushion.

Even writing the Torah requires special objects. The *sofer*, scribe, is one whose only task is to write a Torah. He uses a special parchment made from kosher animals, a quill usually made of goose or turkey feathers, and a specially prepared vegetable ink.

Classroom Development

Once again, brainstorming can be effective in motivating students to learn. From the second chapter, students became aware of how important migration is in understanding their family's history as well as Jewish history. It is quite probable that some of your students will be moving with their family or on their own once they have reached adulthood. Those who will be attending college will likely want to experience, if only for a short period, the independence of an "out-of-town college."

Let's begin with college. Tell your students to pretend they are going to attend college in a city (state, country) other than the one in which they are now living. After briefly describing what they may find (most likely a predominantly non-Jewish population) explain that they will be permitted to take with them *one* trunk (perhaps a camp trunk). Ask each student to make a list of those Jewish items he or she will take.

Allow each student an opportunity to explain to the class why each item was selected. A short writing experience could follow:

1. "The things I hold dear."
2. "What my (grandfather, grandmother, parent) left for me."
3. "When I hold my (grandfather's, father's) kiddish cup, I . . ."
4. "The Shabbat candlesticks my mother uses reminds me . . ."
5. "If only I hadn't thrown away the . . ."

The short essays can be read in class. They can later be displayed on the class bulletin board and/or included in the class newspaper or magazine.

Suggested Classroom and Homework Activities

1. Ask your students to tell the story of a family photograph which they have brought to class. Family photographs are an important and exciting part of family history study. It is enriching to see pictures of ancestors, their families, and of Holocaust victims whose pictures may exist. Since old photographs are among people's most precious possessions, originals *should not* be brought to class. They can be copied by taking a photograph of them. A .35mm camera and a close-up lens are needed. The photograph should be set on a flat surface and sufficient lighting should be available. A tripod will keep the camera steady. Even without a close-up lens, a photograph of a photograph can be made. Also, if details and shading are not necessary, a photocopy of a photograph will do.

2. Have the class visit the synagogue's sanctuary. Invite an older congregant to accompany you to explain how the various ritual objects came to be part of the synagogue's worship service.
3. Ask your students to tell the story of one ritual object that they have brought from home to class.
4. Many immigrants coming to America by steamship during the early part of the twentieth century saw a "wireless" radio for the first time. The "wireless" was only one of the new inventions our ancestors "discovered" when they came to America. What other "discoveries" did our ancestors make when they came to America? See duplicating master #13.
5. Jewish life is filled with a rich mixture of various kinds of religious and cultural customs, many of which require ritual objects. Just about every Jewish holiday has a unique set of ritual objects to go with it. Duplicating master #14 will help your students identify some ritual objects and the occasions when they are used.
6. Your students may want to prepare a class joke book made up of favorite family jokes. (See page 77 in *My Generations*.) Duplicating master #15 provides your students with the opportunity to write favorite family jokes for a class joke book.
7. On page 75 in *My Generations* there is space for your students to write favorite family sayings. Conduct a poster contest in class in which each student is asked to design and draw a poster that illustrates the family saying to be written at the bottom of the poster.

Chapter 5 at a glance:

Activities in My Generations:

1. Family Heirlooms (p. 61)
2. Our Oldest Books (p. 63)
3. Family Photographs (pp. 65–67)
4. Family Documents (p. 69)
5. Family Documents (pp. 71–73)
6. Family Sayings (p. 75)
7. Favorite Family Stories (p. 76)
8. Family Jokes (p. 77)
9. Family Pets (p. 78)

Duplicating Masters:

1. New In Their Lifetime (#13)
2. Holidays And Their Ritual Objects (#14)
3. Favorite Family Jokes (#15)

CHAPTER 6

BECOMING A BAR/BAT MITZVAH

Aims of the Chapter

To portray the bar/bat mitzvah as a significant step in a person's growth and development as a Jew. To characterize the bar/bat mitzvah as a link to generations. To assess the importance to Jewish tradition—and survival—of the relationship between a teacher and a student.

Jewish Values

1. The love of and respect for learning are instilled early and regularly in the Jewish home.
2. The coming of age for Jewish youth is marked by reading Torah. The young are then obligated to assume responsibility for their *own* education: At thirteen he is ready for Mitzvot (Avot 5:2) *and* He who takes upon himself the yoke of Torah, will find the yoke of the world removed from him (Avot 3:6).
3. Teachers and students are equal links on the chain of Jewish education. The weakness of one will sap the strength of the other.

Background

Tradition of Bar/Bat Mitzvah

The Torah does not mention the Bar or Bat Mitzvah. It is not until Talmudic times that there is evidence of the age of thirteen being a milestone in a Jew's life. The Talmud says that if someone over the age of thirteen makes a vow, he is bound by it. The Talmud also reveals that when a boy is thirteen (and when a girl is twelve) he is obligated to fast on Yom Kippur.

"Bar Mitzvah" means "son of" (bar) "[the] commandment" (mitzvah). In the *Ethics of the Fathers*, it is written: "At age 13, one becomes subject to the commandments" (Avot 5:21). Custom has given to us the Bar (and Bat) Mitzvah. The adolescent must now be responsible for his or her religious life.

In Genesis Rabbah, the rabbis discuss Isaac's sons, Jacob and Esau. Rabbi Eleazar b. R. Simeon says, "A man is responsible for his son until the age of thirteen, thereafter he must say, 'Blessed is He who now freed me from the responsibility of this boy'" (63:10). It is traditional that a father says the prayer on the day of his son's Bar Mitzvah. According to tradition, for the first thirteen years of a child's life, his sins are the responsibility of his father. After thirteen, he is on his own. While the boy is still the *son* of the father, he is now the *son of the commandments*. No longer is the father the authority; now it is the commandments of the Torah.

The actual term, Bar Mitzvah, first appears in Jewish literature in the Middle Ages, and the customs we currently observe are probably about 700 years old. So while the idea of the age of thirteen as an important milestone is quite old, the actual ritual we observe is much more recent.

A Bar Mitzvah celebration can take place on Monday or Thursday, as well as Shabbat. These are the days when the Torah is read publicly.

The Aliyah

Being called to the Torah for an aliyah is considered a great honor among Jews. The word *aliyah* which means "going up" is a time when one is called *up* to read from the Torah. That same word, *aliyah*, is used today in reference to making one's home in the State of Israel. Since living in Israel has been seen traditionally as a mitzvah, we call it *going up*.

There are four different kinds of aliyot which a Bar/Bat Mitzvah can receive.

First is a regular aliyah before the reading of the Torah. The person recites the blessings before and after the Torah reading while someone else reads the scroll.

Second is an aliyah where the Bar/Bat Mitzvah recites the blessings and *also* reads the Torah passage. The celebrant is given the *last* part of the weekly reading known as the *maftir*. Maftir means *one who concludes*. Traditionally, this last aliyah has the greatest honor attached to it.

In the third kind of aliyah, the Bar or Bat Mitzvah reads the entire Torah portion for the week.

Finally, the Bar or Bat Mitzvah recites the *Haftarah*.

The Service

The word haftarah means *completion* and refers to the readings from the book of Prophets in the Bible. Every Torah portion has a corresponding portion from the Prophets. This is read on Shabbat. Throughout the world, when a certain part of the Torah is read, a specific portion from the Prophets is also read. This custom is mentioned in the Talmud.

Some children who are Bar/Bat Mitzvah lead the entire service on that day of celebration. Regardless of what the participation is, the act of being called to join in the Torah service has become the traditional symbol of the Bar/Bat Mitzvah.

Another traditional part of the service is the child's speech on some aspect of Jewish law, often a response to the Torah portion he or she has just chanted. As part of the preparation for the day, the Bar/Bat Mitzvah does research into a certain aspect of Jewish law and *teaches* his or her congregation. The tradition of Torah study is an important part of Jewish life and here, for the first time, the young people have the opportunity to display their abilities in this area.

The Bar/Bat Mitzvah is a *coming of age* ceremony quite unlike those of other people. For Jews, becoming an adult means added responsibility and added learning and Jews celebrate their full participation by studying and reading the Torah. It has become frequent today to hear of adults—many of whom are married with children of their own—studying to become Bar/Bat Mitzvah. While the ages of thirteen and twelve are traditional for beginning, they mark only the beginning and one can become a son or daughter of the covenant at any time during his or her life. The Bar or Bat Mitzvah, however, is *automatic* upon attaining the appropriate age. At any time after thirteen or twelve, while a person may be called to the Torah for the first time, the ceremony is not really a Bar or Bat Mitzvah.

Classroom Development

The following story was written by a student of mine, Seth Bernstein. It is a sensitive portrait of his grandfather and of a world increasingly more alive in memory than in reality. The story also portrays vividly the Bar Mitzvah as a vital link between generations.

Read the story to the class. Afterwards, allow your students to react to the characters, the setting, and the situation. Undoubtedly, many of your students—whether they have become Bar/Bat Mitzvah or not—will find much in the story to relate to.

An overnight stay at grandpa Bernie's house was something to really look forward to when I was a child. Mommy would pack my suitcase late Thursday night in preparation for the early Friday morning train ride to Williamsburg, Brooklyn, where grandpa had lived since immigrating from Europe some forty years before. Williamsburg, like so many other once middle-class areas, had greatly changed in forty years' time. Blocks which once could be called excitingly busy and bustling were now nothing more than over crowded. Neat clusters of web-backed folding chairs, which for so many years had held their places under the many shade trees on grandpa's block had slowly, but undeniably, been replaced by row upon row of filthy, uncovered garbage cans.

Grandpa's three-room apartment echoed the poverty of the street below. His furniture was rickety, and in many cases held together with pieces of string. The floors were covered with inexpensive oil cloth.

Grandpa's kitchen was my favorite room in the house. A small drop leaf table, surrounded by three unmatched chairs, was shoved against the far end of the room; a noisy barber shop clock hung above it. After eating supper on Friday night, Grandpa and I would sit around the kitchen table and just talk over what was on our minds. I would bring him up to date regarding my neighborhood friends; he would fill me in as to who had moved out of his, by now, half-vacant, building. I could discuss anything with my grandpa. He had an infinite amount of patience, coupled with an innate ability to make all my problems seem small. After a cozy night's sleep in my grandpa's big warm bed, I was always greeted by a breakfast consisting of lumpy but ever-so-tasty oatmeal. By mid-morning, my father would come to take me home. My all too short visit with grandpa came to an end.

As the years passed, Grandpa was no longer able to invite me to spend the night at his house. Nonetheless, I still found the time to spend many a Sunday afternoon with him, walking to the park, and talking as we had so many times before. My problems continued to loom large in my mind, yet Grandpa was still able to resolve my difficulties and help me in many ways. My grandfather displayed great pride in me and instilled in me an intense desire for learning. I studied hard and maintained high grades, knowing it would make him proud.

All too quickly the years slipped by and I developed into a young man approaching Bar Mitzvah age. These same years changed my beloved grandpa into a sickly old man. He could no longer take long walks with me but we still sat together talking endlessly and enjoying each other's company. My grandfather expressed the desire to prepare me for my Bar Mitzvah, just as he had done for my father when he was my age. We studied together and when the task was almost entirely accomplished a disaster struck. My grandfather suffered a paralyzing stroke which left him unable to speak. Although his face was twisted, in my eyes he was still beautiful. I sat by his bed reviewing my Bar Mitzvah preparations over and over again and his eyes shone with pleasure and satisfaction. I reassured my grandpa that on the day of my Bar Mitzvah I would even surpass his greatest expectation. Over and over again, I would say, "Wait and see Grandpa, just wait and see."

A week before this momentous occasion my grandfather succumbed to a fatal heart attack. I was heartbroken and cried convulsively at his graveside. My head was racked with pain and my heart was broken. How could one suffer such a tremendous loss and still carry on? My father, standing beside his father's grave, grasped my hand and told me to look up to the sky, and assured me that things would be brighter and life had to go on.

The morning of my Bar Mitzvah I had a dull sick aching feeling within me. Although I was totally prepared for the ceremony, I was quite apprehensive. As I scanned the crowded room, I noticed the looks of love mixed with anticipation upon the faces of my closest relatives. How I wished my grandpa were with me now to share in my joy! As I began chanting my Bar Mitzvah portion, my voice quavered. Suddenly, within me, I heard my grandpa reciting along with me, just as he had done over and over again during most of my long year of preparation. Suddenly, a feeling of self-confidence overcame me, and as my voice grew stronger and calmer, I realized that my grandpa was indeed with me, as he would always be.

A short writing experience could follow:

1. "What I remember most about my Bar/Bat Mitzvah."
2. "The relative I met for the first time at my Bar/Bat Mitzvah."
3. "The relative who wasn't there at my Bar/Bat Mitzvah."
4. "The relative I want most to be with at my Bar/Bat Mitzvah is . . ."
5. "Why I am/am not looking forward to my Bar/Bat Mitzvah."
6. "What is most important to me about my Bar/Bat Mitzvah."

These short essays can be read in class. They can later be displayed on the class bulletin board and/or included in the class newspaper or magazine.

Suggested Classroom and Homework Activities

1. Ask your students to identify the four Biblical passages written on the parchment scrolls in the two small black boxes of the tefillin (phylacteries) and to explain the reasons for including them (Exodus 13:1–10; Exodus 13:11–16; Deut. 6:4–9; Deut. 11:13–21).

   Bring a set of tefillin to class to demonstrate how it is worn or ask a student to demonstrate its use.

2. Ask some students to prepare an oral report on the origin of the tallit in the Bible (Numbers 15:37–40) and its reflection of the dress Jews wore during Biblical times. Other students may be asked to prepare a report on some of the customs associated with the making and wearing of the tallit. Be sure to bring a tallit to class for this discussion.

3. Ask students to prepare oral reports on their Haftarah portion *and* Torah portion read on the day of their Bar or Bat Mitzvah.

4. Ask students to bring to class a photograph of a relative taken on the day of his or her Bar or Bat Mitzvah and to tell the story of that person's experience.

5. Do your students know the history of their synagogue? Duplicating master #16 offers some questions for them to answer.

6. How well do your students know their rabbi or what the role of the rabbi is in a modern Jewish congregation? Duplicating master #17 offers some questions for their rabbi to answer in an interview.

Chapter 6 at a glance:

Activities in My Generations:

1. My Bar/Bat Mitzvah (p. 80)
2. Family Bar/Bat Mitzvah Record (p. 81)
3. My Bar/Bat Mitzvah Speech (pp. 82–83)
4. My Teachers (p. 84)
5. My Family Bar/Bat Mitzvah Photographs (pp. 86–87)
6. Family Education Record (pp. 88–89)
7. Family Synagogue Memberships (p. 90)

Duplicating Masters:

1. My Congregation's History (#16)
2. Tell Me, Rabbi (#17)

CHAPTER 7

WHAT ARE YOU GOING TO BE?

Aims of the Chapter

To sketch the process of selecting a career. To outline the kinds of occupations Jews have had in recent history. To stress that while our ancestors' work experiences may not be unique, the process of digging out stories about their experiences and listening to them can be exciting and rewarding. To show that Jews often organized into groups based on their professions.

Jewish Values

1. The Talmud teaches that it is a parent's responsibility to teach his child a trade.
2. The individual's acceptance of responsibility for the welfare of his or her neighbors is evident in the number and scope of social service and benevolent organizations in the Jewish community.

Background

Work in the Bible

The first reference to work in the Bible is Genesis. The first "worker" of course is God, who created the heavens and the earth and all living creatures. And though God created man and woman to work (rule) over the living creatures, the *first* human worker was Adam: "The Lord God took the man and placed him in the Garden of Eden, to till it and tend it" (Gen. 2:15).

Later, we find our first shepherd, Abel, and our second farmer, Cain: "Abel became a keeper of sheep, and Cain became a tiller of the soil" (Gen. 4:1). After Cain kills Abel, he is banished to become a ceaseless wanderer, exiled from his home *and* his occupation (Gen. 4:13). The Patriarchs, too, were nomads while Moses and David, like Abel, were shepherds.

Perhaps the most famous hunter in the Bible was Esau: "When the boys grew up, Esau became a skillful hunter, a man of the outdoors; but Jacob was a mild man, who stayed in camp" (Gen. 25:27). We know that Isaac favored Esau, his first born and, therefore, the one to be given the birthright *and* that Rebekah favored Jacob. We also know that Esau *sold* his birthright to Jacob who thought it was more appropriate for him to have the birthright since he was the student and Esau not. The conflict reflected in the Esau and Jacob story between the *dweller* (*farmer, student*) and the *traveler* (nomad, shepherd) is evident throughout the Bible.

The Eastern European Work Experience

Unfortunately, the post-Biblical history of Jewish occupations and the history of anti-Semitism go hand in hand. Many official acts of anti-Semitism were economic in nature. At different times in different places throughout history, Jews were subjected to harsh economic oppression. Sometimes this consisted of not being permitted to own land. Other times, Jews were restricted from certain professions altogether.

Most families in Eastern Europe were involved in any number of trades and skills. These included the buying and selling of wares, blacksmithing, cap making, shopkeeping, and so on. Jews were also innkeepers. Jewish taverns were popular spots for Jews and non-Jews alike.

Even when Jews were forbidden to own land, many were farmers, leasing the land and producing some crop on it. Some Jews, while unable to own a farm, would still own cows and sell the milk products. Tevye the dairyman, the famous character by Sholem Aleichem, is a good example of this profession.

But it would be easy and inaccurate to generalize about the history of Jewish professional life in Eastern Europe. Since not all Jews lived in small towns, and since not all Jews lived in Eastern Europe (many lived in Western Europe, or the Middle East, or elsewhere), one could hardly think of a profession which was not within the experience of some Jews somewhere.

The American-Jewish Work Experience

One of the ironies of history is that while Jews were restricted from many professions in so many places in Eastern Europe, it actually resulted in an advantage when they arrived in the United States. Think of it this way: a non-Jewish farmer, arriving in New York City in 1908 would have a more difficult time adapting to the environment than a Jewish tailor or shopkeeper. With a little saved money, a Jewish shopkeeper could open a store and perhaps build a thriving business. Some of the major department stores in the United States—stores like Abraham and Straus, Fortunoff's, and Macy's—started as small shops run by Jewish immigrants. One of the largest men's shirt manufacturing companies in the United States, Van Huesen, is owned and operated by the Phillips family, a Jewish family from Suwalki in Poland.

Another important factor to mention regarding how well Jews adapted to life in America is education. For literally thousands of years, Jews have emphasized education. In fact, the very first example of universal education for children is recorded in the Talmud. Jewish children, over 2000 years ago, were required by Jewish law to be taught to read and write.

One rarely hears of a Jew going to a university in Eastern Europe—although this did happen sometimes. But usually a child went to a Jewish school, a *heder* and then, perhaps, to a state school for a while. But degrees in higher education were quite a luxury in Europe.

The use of the mind has always been a high priority among Jews. Therefore, when Jews arrived in the United States, they took advantage of the freedom of opportunity and pursued careers which often required degrees in higher education. For the last sixty years, children of Jewish immigrants to America have constituted the highest percentage of college-educated young people, higher than any other immigrant group.

Classroom Development

As we saw in Chapter 1 of this guide, role playing can be an effective teaching tool. Here it can be successful in helping students gain insight into the process of making decisions about a career. Some students may have had some experience in this area as a result of part-time, after-school jobs or summer employment.

Again, allow your students time before engaging in the role playing to think about the roles they will play. Have two children act as reporters to write a brief news story of the events (or assign two students to each event). Allow the performers to react first to their own performances and then have the reporters and the rest of the class react.

Here are several situations in which the student can gain insight into the process of making decisions about a career:

1. A father wants his son to take over his business but the son has a different career in mind.
2. A young man or woman must convince a skeptical prospective employer that he or she is right for the job now available in the employer's firm.
3. A young man or woman is a supervisor of several workers. His or her boss has told the supervisor that a worker must be fired and that it is the supervisor's job to do the firing.
4. A father refuses to support his daughter's decision to go to college instead of business school. He wants her to work only until she gets married and then she will work as a housewife and mother. The girl's mother disagrees. She has been harboring resentment toward her husband because he has never encouraged her to seek job fulfillment outside the home.
5. A young man or woman tries to settle an argument between his or her father and grandfather over the best possible career for the young person.

You may want to begin with a *word association* game before introducing the role playing activity. Remember, unlike brainstorming, word association calls for rapid-fire responses of one, two, or, at most, three words. Write the responses on the board as the students call them out (or, have a student act as secretary). Work around the room calling for a response to each word from each student.

Ask for responses to the following words:

plumber	business school	blue collar	white collar
college	teacher	rabbi	salary
doctor	fringe benefit	secretary	vacation
graduation	diploma	lawyer	unemployment
cantor	butcher	9–5	social security
job interview		union	electrician

A short writing experience could follow:

1. "When I grow up, I want to be . . . "
2. "When I grow up, I don't want to be . . . "
3. "I want a job that will allow me to . . . "
4. "The job my (father, mother) has . . . "
5. "The most successful person I know . . . "
6. "What is most satisfying about doing a *good* job . . . "
7. "When I retire, I want to be able to say . . . "

The short essays can be read in class. They can later be displayed on the class bulletin board and/or included in the class newspaper or magazine.

Suggested Classroom and Homework Activities

1. It is fascinating to learn about the professions of our ancestors. Ask your students to tell a story about an ancestor's job that has had a permanent influence on their *picture* of that ancestor.

2. Invite a synagogue employee (cantor, caretaker, secretary, president) or a parent or grandparent to be interviewed about the work he or she does or has done: *career exploration*. (See fact sheet, "Tell Me, Rabbi," duplicating master #17.)

3. Have your students ask their parents: "How would your professional goals have changed had your parents (grandparents) not immigrated to the United States?" Ask each student to prepare a report for oral presentation.

4. The *Jewish Daily Forward*, a Yiddish newspaper in America, began publication in 1897 and

is still publishing today, although now as a weekly. The newspaper played an important role in helping East European Jewish immigrants adjust to American life. One popular feature was *The Bintel Brief*, letters to the editor. One of the major difficulties immigrants faced was in employment. Sample letters from *The Bintel Brief* are offered in duplicating master #18.

5. Many observers of Jewish history and the Jewish community in America today note that Jewish life has always been rich with organizations. Duplicating master #19 lists many of the major ones. Ask your students to prepare an oral report on the organizations their parents and grandparents belong to and *why* they are members.
6. Ask students to prepare a brief oral report on the tragic Triangle Shirtwaist Factory fire of 1911.

Chapter 7 at a glance:

Activities in My Generations:

1. My Ancestors' Occupations (p. 93)
2. Photographs of My Ancestors' Occupations (p. 85)
3. Stories About My Ancestors' Occupations (p. 96)
4. Parents' Occupational History (p. 97)
5. Organizations We Joined (p. 99)

Duplicating Masters:

1. A Bintel Brief: All About Working (#18)
2. Jewish Organizations (#19)

CHAPTER 8

WHEN YOU GET MARRIED

Aims of the Chapter

To portray the wedding ceremony as an ancient Jewish rite that connects generations. To assess the value and significance of the *ketubah*, the Jewish marriage contract. To stress that the wedding ceremony unites the couple in the eyes of God *and* in the eyes of the Jewish community.

Jewish Values

1. Companionship is the principal reason for marriage: "The Lord God said, 'It is not good for man to be alone; I will make a fitting helper for him'" (Gen. 2:15).
2. Having children is an important reason for marriage: "And God created man in His image, in the image of God He created him; male and female He created them. God blessed them and God said to them 'Be fertile and increase . . .'" (Gen 1:27–28).
3. The family is the foundation upon which all of Jewish life is built.
4. *Shalom Bayit*, peace in the home, is a goal to which all family members must aspire.

Background

Marriage in the Bible

At a boy's b'rit, the assemblage chants: "As he has entered the covenant, so may he enter Torah, marriage, and good deeds."

The first Biblical reference to the union between man and woman occurs early in Genesis: "And God created man in His image, in the image of God He created him; male and female He created them. God blessed them and God said to them, 'Be fertile and increase, fill the earth and master it; and rule the fish of the sea, the birds of the sky, and all the living things that creep on earth'" (Gen. 1:27–28).

"Be fertile and increase" is the first mitzvah in the Torah, but it was for companionship that God first created man and woman, that they should be together: "It is not good for man to be alone" (Gen. 2:15).

In Biblical times, it was the practice for a man to have more than one wife, and a number of concubines (a woman without the status of a wife). The man, however, could not commit incest or adultery, that is, have sexual relations with a married woman who was not his wife or concubine (Deut. 22:13–24:1; Lev. 18:1–30; Lev. 20:10–27).

The Get

The bill of divorcement allowed a woman to remarry and was most often granted a man when a marriage produced no children. The *get* or bill of divorcement in the Talmud (still in use today among many Jews) is based on the Biblical tradition of divorce. Today, the *get* is more a protection for the woman: without it she could not remarry according to Jewish law.

The Jewish Marriage

Traditionally, a Jewish marriage begins with an engagement. While not unlike modern day engagements celebrated by Jews and non-Jews, a Jewish engagement is also a legal matter, though this aspect is not required.

Today, the Jewish wedding actually begins on the Shabbat before the wedding day itself. At this time, the groom is called to the Torah for an aliyah. (In some congregations, both the bride and the groom are called up.) This is a tradition going back to Biblical times. Because the congregation of friends and relatives desire the wedding to be a *sweet* one, it is popular custom to toss candy and raisins in the direction of the groom (or bride and groom) to concretely represent this wish. The name of this entire Shabbat experience is *aufruf*.

On the wedding day itself, the bride and groom traditionally fast until the ceremony. Similar to the Yom Kippur feast, fasting on a wedding day helps the couple to approach their marriage in a serious and thoughtful mood. For while a wedding is a time for joy and celebration, it is also a *sacred connection* between two living souls. The fast also serves as a *cleansing*, helping to purify the bride and groom before they enter into a new life.

The signing of the ketubah often takes place before the marriage ceremony itself, but it is traditional for it to occur under the huppah. The huppah, or canopy, held over the bride and groom during the wedding, is a symbol of the new home they will create together.

While it is currently popular for a husband and wife to exchange rings, according to Jewish tradition, it is the custom for the groom to give a ring to the bride. This symbolic act can be seen as the groom's expression of his obligation to his bride. It is customary for the bride to walk around the groom several times. This, too, is symbolic: it is a way for the bride to express her obligation to the groom.

During the wedding ceremony itself, certain words are spoken. Traditionally, the groom recites his obligations. In recent years, the bride has done the same.

Standing under the huppah, looking at his bride, the groom recites the words, "Behold you are consecrated to me with this ring according to the laws of Moses and the People of Israel." These are the same words spoken by our ancestors at their weddings. This sentence is a public statement to the bride and to all present that the marriage is sealed. It is at this point in the ceremony that the two witnesses sign the ketubah. Jewish law requires two witnesses when a contract is signed and a wedding is no exception.

At the end of the wedding ceremony, a glass is broken, usually by the groom, who steps on it, shattering it. There are many meanings which can be read into this gesture, one being that just as a shattered glass is now permanently in that condition, so, too, will the new husband and wife be a permanent couple.

After the ceremony itself, the bride and groom participate privately in a ritual called *yihud*. The custom grew out of the idea that at this time the couple would make love (which is the *profound joining*). In recent generations, the couple break their fast at this time and have a few private moments together before joining the wedding feast.

The obligations of the bride and groom are complete after the ritual of *yihud*, and then it is time for the wedding guests to meet their obligations. In Jewish tradition, the wedding guests must fulfill the obligation of *m'sameakh hatan v'kallah*, of causing the bride and groom to rejoice. It is a fundamental Jewish obligation for the guests to bring additional joy. The custom of lifting the bride and groom on chairs and dancing with them is part of the mitzvah of rejoicing with them.

Every effort is made to create a meaningful marriage ceremony. But while a wedding is approached with a sense of permanence, divorce is permitted—and even encouraged—under certain circumstances by Jewish tradition. (The Talmud relates that God Himself cries when there is a divorce.) Sometimes couples who are married recognize that the healthiest thing to do is to break the bonds of the marriage.

Jewish tradition does not require a couple to live together unhappily. A Jewish divorce represents a deep sensitivity to the human condition. We enter marriage with hopes and dreams, but we are aware that as there is a union, so, too, is there a separation.

Classroom Development

Though marriage may be the Biblical and Talmudic ideal, in our present society marriage has "taken a beating" and so has family life. Each year, you will find in your classroom more children from "broken homes"; most will be living with their mothers, visiting their fathers on weekends. You will also find more young people talking about delaying marriage until they are settled in their careers or until they have "seen the world." Intermarriage and interdating is also on the rise.

While you may want to discuss marriage and its importance to the future of world Jewry, you need also to be sensitive to the needs and circumstances of your students. A good way to begin here is with what the *students bring to class themselves*. Brainstorming, as we have seen earlier, is a nonthreatening approach to a subject.

Write the words "a *husband* is" and "a *wife* is" on the board and ask your students to give brief definitions. Write the definitions as the students call them out (or have a student act as secretary). Do this also with the following: "a *marriage* is"; "a *wedding ceremony* is"; "a *honeymoon* is."

After the board is filled, point to a definition such as: "a *husband* is one partner in a marriage" and ask your students a question such as: "*How* is a husband a partner in a marriage?" or "*What* are some of the responsibilities a husband should share with his wife?" Point to another definition such as: "a *wedding ceremony* is the occasion for family and friends to be part of the joy the bride and groom experience" or "a *wedding ceremony* is that time when a couple pays their respect to God" and ask the students a question such as: "*Why* should family and friends be invited to a wedding?" or "*Why* should God be part of a wedding ceremony?"

A short writing experience could follow:

1. "What I think about when I think about being a parent."
2. "The personal qualities a parent should have."
3. "Why I (agree, disagree) with zero population growth."
4. "How I would plan my wedding."
5. "When my grandparents were married."
6. "What I would include in my marriage contract."
7. "The best time to get married."
8. "The family in the year 2084."

The short essays can be read in class. They may later be displayed on the class bulletin board and/or included in the class newspaper or magazine.

Suggested Classroom and Homework Activities

1. Ask students to bring to class a wedding photograph of relatives and tell the story of their wedding.
2. Ask students to read the story of Rebekah's betrothal (Gen. 24:1–67) and prepare an oral report which includes answers to the following questions: a) What were Rebekah's

qualities that endeared her so to Isaac that he wanted to marry her? b) What qualities will you look for in a partner when you are ready for marriage?

3. The Jewish wedding has a unique set of ritual objects and customs to go with it. What are they? (See duplicating master #20.)

4. Many letters were written to the *Jewish Daily Forward's* "A Bintel Brief" column on the subject of marriage. Read the following letter to your students. Ask each to share marriage superstitions they may know.

1908
Dear Editor,

I ask you to give me some advice in my situation. I am a young man of twenty-five, sixteen years in America, and I recently met a fine girl. She has a flaw, however, that keeps me from marrying her. The fault is that she has a dimple in her chin, and it is said that people who have this lose their first husband or wife.

At first I laughed at the idea, but later it began to bother me. I began to observe people with dimpled chins and found out that their first husbands or wives really had died prematurely. I got so interested in this that whenever I see someone with this defect I ask about it immediately, and I find out that some of the men have lost their first wives, and some of the women's first husbands are dead.

This upset me so that I don't know what to do. I can't leave my sweetheart. I love her very much. But I'm afraid to marry her lest I die because of the dimple. I've questioned many people. Some say it's true, others laugh at the idea.

Perhaps you, too, will laugh at me for being such a fool and believing such nonsense, but I cannot rest until I hear your opinion about it. I want to add that my sweetheart knows nothing about this.

Respectfully,
The Unhappy Fool

You may want to ask your students to respond to the letter writer before reading the *Forward's* response.

Answer:

The tragedy is not that the girl has a dimple in her chin but that some people have a screw loose in their heads! One would need the knowledge of a genius to explain how a dimple in the chin could drive a husband or wife to the grave. Does the angel of death sit hiding in the dimple? It seems to us that it is a beauty spot, and we never imagined it could house the Devil.

It's tragic humor to find such superstition in the world today. It's truly shameful that a young man who was brought up in America should ask such questions. To calm him, we wish to tell him we know many people with such dimples who have not lost their first husbands or wives, but live out their years together in great happiness.

5. "A Bintel Brief" also printed many letters on *matchmaking*. What do you think about this practice? Duplicating master #21 provides the text of a letter on the subject. After the students read the letter, lead a discussion on what *their* advice would be. Here is the answer provided by the *Forward* in 1930:

Answer:

It depends on how a person feels about this, because consulting a matchmaker has nothing to do with education or enlightenment. One person might consider it like a fair where cattle are sold. Another person has an altogether different opinion because a shadkhan nowadays does not match up brides and grooms sight unseen. He just introduces people so that they can get acquainted. If they like each other they can fall in love. Couldn't the parks, Coney Island beaches, or a dance hall where people meet, also be considered matchmakers?

Chapter 8 at a glance:

Activities in My Generations:

1. My Parents' Ketubah (p. 103)
2. My Grandparents' Ketubah (pp. 105–106)
3. Family Weddings (pp. 108–109)
4. My Grandparents' Wedding Photographs (p. 111)
5. My Parents' Wedding Photograph (p. 112)
6. Family Wedding Photographs (pp. 113–114)

Duplicating Masters:

1. The Jewish Wedding (#20)
2. Matchmaker, Matchmaker (#21)

CHAPTER 9

VISITING A JEWISH CEMETERY

Aims of the Chapter

To emphasize that a cemetary is not a place to avoid, that it is a sign of respect and love to visit the graves of loved ones. To note the several times during a year when Jews will visit the graves of loved ones. To characterize cemeteries as monuments to memories. To demonstrate that inscriptions on memorial stones link generations.

Jewish Values

1. Jewish tradition treasures life; however, it recognizes the inevitability of death: "For dust you are, and to dust you shall return" (Gen. 3:19).
2. The dignity of the deceased is maintained by following the religious laws and customs regarding death and mourning.
3. Memorial stones reflect respect for the dead and consecrate their burial place.

Background

Burial Practices

Cemeteries play an important part in Jewish life. They are as important for the living as for the dead: it is the living who erect the gravestone and it is the living who decide what words should be engraved on the stone; it is the living who visit the grave and it is the living who read the words on the stone each visit.

Jewish burial practices have been with us ever since the beginning of our recorded history: "And Jacob set up a monument upon her grave and this is the monument of Rachel's grave to this very day" (Gen. 35:20). Our earliest patriarchs observed the custom of setting up a tombstone.

There have been many kinds of Jewish burial places. In our early history, burials took place in caves. Later, this custom disappeared, but we have always been conscious of the importance of arranging a place to bury our dead: "Sell me a burial site." (Gen. 23:4). These words were spoken by Abraham when he arranged to set up a burial place for his family. One of the first things Jewish immigrants did when they arrived in America was to purchase property to establish burial plots. The first organizations they formed were *burial societies* which aided members by providing their families with burial plots. Unfortunately, our cemeteries, sacred as they are to us, have often been desecrated. History records the destruction of Jewish cemeteries as early as the Middle Ages, and today we still hear of Jewish graveyards attacked by vandals.

When Jews die, they are buried as soon as possible—usually the day after death with the exceptions of the Sabbath and Jewish Festivals. Also, short delays of a day or two are permitted when a close relative needs to travel a long distance to attend the funeral.

Special rituals occur after a death. The body is never left alone between the death and the burial. Also, the body is washed. The body is then clothed in a white robe. This simple garment is worn to show that in the eyes of God, rich and poor are alike. Traditionally, the male is wrapped in his tallit. The coffin is simple and must be made of wood.

Jews *do not* display an open coffin at a funeral. It is believed that to view a deceased person in an open coffin does the deceased a dishonor. Two other practices which Jews *do not* follow are cremations and autopsies. These are forbidden by Jewish law.

There are other traditions Jews observe on the occasion of a death. Ever since Biblical times, Jews have torn the garment they wore when they heard about a death of a close relative, and this act is a symbolic sign of grief and mourning. The torn garment is traditionally worn throughout the week of mourning—*shiva*—except on the Sabbath. When the garment is torn, a special prayer is said: "Blessed are Thou, Lord our God, the true Judge."

Memorial stones are usually placed at the head of a grave a year after the burial. Though tradition has not set a required time, the *one-year* custom is based on the fact that during the first year after death, the mourners say *kaddish*, the traditional prayer for the dead, every day. It is only after the year is over and kaddish is no longer said that the *need* to erect a monument arises. Until then, the deceased is remembered every day. Usually in America, the memorial stone is erected at a special occasion called an *unveiling*. Again, this is not required by Jewish law, but it has come to be a time when special tributes are made for the deceased. The stone is erected and the family visits the grave site along with friends.

Cemetery Plots

There are four types of plots in a Jewish cemetery: 1) family plots, where members of a family are buried close to one another; 2) synagogue plots, which are owned by a congregation for use by its members; 3) Landsmannschaften plots, which are owned by a group of people who came from the same town or region in Europe; 4) individual plots, which are owned by people who do not use an organization's plot.

As you walk through a Jewish cemetery, Jewish symbols appear in all directions. On the more ornate tombstones, you will see a variety of Jewish symbols as part of the monument. Throughout Jewish history, a number of symbols have come to be traditional, the Star of David perhaps the most famous. Examining other tombstones, you will see other symbols as well. One may be the two hands that symbolize a member of a Priestly family—*Kohanim*. Or you may see a menorah, a lion's image, or some other artwork. Jewish art is a part of Jewish cemeteries.

And Jewish cemeteries are another important link in the chain of generations.

Classroom Development

Once again, we have a subject that may cause our students discomfort and anxiety. Remember that although the subject is cemeteries and what we can learn from burial practices about our family history, your students may not be able to separate *death* from the genealogical pursuit. It is vital to the success of this aspect of gathering family history that you not deny the very strong feelings some may have about this subject—whether it be burial practices or death. You need to be sensitive, once more, to the needs and circumstances of your students. Don't push those who are resistant but *do* encourage those who want to participate fully. If necessary, invite the rabbi to speak to your class about death and mourning but only *if necessary*. As the teacher, *you* must not lose sight of the subject!

In Chapter 2, the students were asked to answer the question: *Whom do I see when I see me?* Now you want them to answer this question: *Whom will they see when they see me?* Tell your students to imagine that they have reached the Biblical age of 120 years, the end of their lives. What will their obituaries say? Here are some points they may want to include:

Name
Cause of death
Survived by
Occupation
Major accomplishments
Memberships in
Goals reached and not reached
Will be remembered most for
Burial will be at
In lieu of flowers, contributions may be made to

The next assignment is to write his or her epitaph. *What will be engraved on your tombstone?* Some students may want to design their stones. They should be allowed to. For those who think the activity is *morbid*, emphasis should be placed on the fact that they are engaging in the activity *in life*. Though the inevitability of death is certain to be mentioned, it need not be dwelled upon.

A short writing experience could follow:

1. "My world and welcome to it."
2. "The last funeral I attended."
3. "There is too much emphasis on death in America."
4. "The first time I became aware of death."
5. "What I remember most about a relative who has died."
6. "How television and movies portray funerals."
7. "The first time I visited a cemetery."
8. "The last time I visited a cemetery."

These essays can be read in class. They may be displayed later on the bulletin board and/or included in the class newspaper or magazine. The obituaries and epitaphs may also be included in these publications.

Suggested Classroom and Homework Activities

1. Invite a local funeral director to class. At the same time, you may want to invite your rabbi to discuss Jewish burial practices.
2. Visit a local cemetery. Ask interested students to do a tombstone rubbing. The procedure is simple and requires only a piece of paper and a pencil. Rubbings and photographs of tombstones can be significant additions to your students' family history collections. Students should prepare an oral report on their experience.
3. Cemeteries, through their tombstones, represent the history of a people. How well do your students know the significance of what is written on a tombstone? Duplicating master #22 provides each student with a drawing of an actual tombstone. In the following excerpt from Arthur Kurzweil's book, *From Generation to Generation*, everything you need to know in order to read a Jewish tombstone is explained. On the basis of this information, the student will be able to decipher the contents of the stone on duplicating master #22 and will learn how to read a Jewish tombstone.
4. It is quite possible that each student's family has a cemetery plot, perhaps one for each side of the family. Ask your students to find out the names of the cemeteries where their

ancestors are buried and their locations. If they have an opportunity to visit a cemetery with their family, they may want to make a tombstone rubbing and report on the experience.

5. Jews are traditionally divided into three groups: the *Kohanim* or priests; the *Levites* or helpers of the kohanim; and the *Israelites*, the rest of the population. Ask your students to prepare an oral report on the role of each in ancient Israel and the role of each in traditional Judaism today.
6. An *ethical will* is a special kind of will written by an individual in *preparation* for death. See duplicating master #23.
7. Memorial books or *yizkor* books are local histories of Jewish communities in Eastern Europe. They can be a valuable source of information for family historians. For a bibliography of these books write for a copy of the Fall 1979–Winter 1980 issue of *Toledot*. (See "Genealogist's Bookshelf," p. 51)
8. It is probable that some children in your class are grandchildren or great-grandchildren of Holocaust survivors or victims. They may want to engage in Holocaust research. It would be helpful to you to read the chapter on this subject in Arthur Kurzweil's *From Generation to Generation*. You may want to introduce the subject by discussing the work of Yad Vashem, Israel's Holocaust memorial and resource center and the "page of testimony."

   At Yad Vashem, there is a section called the Hall of Names. In the Hall of Names is the Pages of Testimony department. Duplicating master #24 provides you with a blank copy of an official page of testimony. Students can fill out the forms, indicating information about people in their families who were murdered. The students can send these forms to Yad Vashem or your class can do this as a group project. Inform your students that their forms will remain forever as testimony about their families. When visiting Yad Vashem, one can see the forms in their files. Write to Yad Vashem at:

   Yad Vashem
   P.O.B. 84
   Jerusalem, Israel

How to Read a Jewish Tombstone

If a tombstone of interest is written in Hebrew (as most Jewish tombstones are—in part, if not completely), a few pointers will be helpful if you cannot read the language.

At the top of most Jewish tombstones is the abbreviation פ"נ for a man and פ"ט for a woman, meaning "here lies" and "here is interred."

At the close of most Jewish tombstone inscriptions you will find the abbreviation תנצבה which stands for a verse from I Sam. 25:29, "May his soul be bound up in the bond of eternal life."

The tombstone may contain an epitaph in Hebrew, in which case you would simply have to copy the letters or take a clear photograph of the inscription and get it translated.

Calculating a date from the Hebrew on the tombstone will also be necessary. Actually, it would be useful for you to learn how to convert a Hebrew date into an English date for tombstones as well as any other Jewish document written in Hebrew. The system is quite simple.

The letters of the Hebrew alphabet each have a numerical value. They are:

א – 1	ז – 7	מ – 40	ק – 100
ב – 2	ח – 8	נ – 50	ר – 200
ג – 3	ט – 9	ס – 60	ש – 300
ד – 4	י – 10	ע – 70	ת – 400
ה – 5	כ – 20	פ – 80	
ו – 6	ל – 30	צ – 90	

When a Hebrew date is written, you must figure out the numerical value of each letter and then add them up. This is the date. But remember that this is the Hebrew date and not the date we use in daily life. In other words each Rosh Hashanah, which appears on the calendar in September or October, we add a year to the Jewish date. In September, 1979, for example, the Jewish year was 5740. With this information you need only do a little arithmetic to change a Hebrew date to a secular date.

There is just one minor complication. Often a Hebrew date after the year 5000 on the Hebrew calendar will leave off the number 5 in the thousands column. In other words, taking the example of 1979 being 5740, you will usually see the Hebrew date written as 740 rather than 5740. To arrive at a Common Era date simply add 1240 to the shortened date. Therefore, 740 plus 1240 is 1980. Why 1980 rather than 1979? Because the Jewish date changes, as I have said, in September or October. Most of the year 5740 will be in 1980, not 1979.

Of course a tombstone as well as other documents will have the month too, probably the Hebrew months. Here is a list of them:

Tishre	September
Heshvan	October
Kislev	November
Tevet	December
Shevat	January
Adar (Adar II in leap year)	February
Nisan	March
Iyar	April
Sivan	May
Tamuz	June
Av	July
Elul	August

Since the Hebrew calendar is not the same as the calendar which we use in secular life, the months indicated above do not correspond exactly. In a given year the corresponding months can be off by several days or even weeks.

Here is one example of how to convert a Hebrew date into an English date: If the year is ת רפ, the letter ת is 400, the letter ר is 200, פ is 80. In total 680. As I pointed out, the 5000 is usually left off, so actually the date would be 5680. But using our formula, 680 plus 1240 is 1920. That is the date we are familiar with.

Chapter 9 at a glance:

Activities in My Generations:

1. Family Cemetery Records (pp. 118–119)
2. Family Yahrzeit Record (p. 121)
3. Family Photographs of Holocaust Victims (pp. 124–125)
4. My Relatives Who Perished During the Holocaust (p. 126)

Duplicating Masters:

1. How To Read A Jewish Tombstone (#22)
2. Ethical Wills (#23)
3. Yad Vashem Page Of Testimony (#24)

CHAPTER 10

CONCLUSION

Aims of the Chapter

To learn that life is a series of decisions we make and that each decision balances what we learn from others' and our own judgments. To note the concept of *free will*. To define the characteristics that form an *authentic Jew*. To stress that as one is informed about Jewish tradition, one finds many ideas and activities to enrich one's life and one gains a better understanding of what choices are available.

Jewish Values

1. Each individual is endowed with a *free will* enabling each to think and act for himself or herself.
2. There is *dignity*, *worth*, and *potential* in each individual.
3. The differences that exist among the Jewish people are respected.

Background

Jews believe in *free will*. Each of us decides what to do with our lives: what to think, how to act, what to be. And the decisions we make affect *every* aspect of our lives: where we live, who we live with, where we work, where we travel. In our lives as Jews, we choose which holidays to observe, rituals to practice, books to read, prayers to say. There is no *correct* way to be Jewish. *It is our decision*.

Every family is different. No two families are alike. Some people never marry; others have no children, while some have many, a few, or even one child. Some marriages end in divorce; some people remarry after a divorce or after a spouse has died. Some people are adopted.

Because every family is different, every family history will be different. Your students will have to keep this in mind as they record their Jewish family history. At times they will be able to find more information on one branch of their family than on another. Parts of *My Generations* may not apply to every student's family or to every branch of the family. Encourage your students to adapt this book to their own families, using the book as a tool and keeping in mind that each student and his or her family is *unique*.

Classroom Development

Several teaching tools can be successful here in motivating your students to think about the future.

You can *brainstorm* with your students. Ask students to complete the following sentence: "Thinking about the *future* makes me . . . " Write the answers on the board as the students call them out (or have a student act as secretary). Do this also with the following: "*Tomorrow* will be"; "A Jew *is*"; "Living a *Jewish life* means."

After the board is filled, point to an answer such as: "Thinking about the *future* makes me *scared*" and ask your students a question such as: "What *scares* you about the future?" or "How can you prepare yourself for the uncertainty of the future?" Point to another answer such as: "Living a *Jewish life* means celebrating the holidays with my family" and ask your students a question such as: "What is your *favorite* Jewish holiday?" or "How do you celebrate Sukkot with your family?"

Role playing can also be used here. Here are several situations in which the students can gain insight into what the future might *mean* to them:

1. A young man/woman leaving home to attend an out-of-state college saying good-bye to his/her family.
2. An American family flying to Israel to make *aliyah*.
3. A young couple talking about the future they want for their newborn son/daughter.
4. A young Israeli man/woman leaving his/her family in Tel Aviv to attend college in the United States.
5. A rabbi talking to a confirmation class about the future he wishes for them.
6. A family reunion.
7. A young man/woman having left home after high school returning home following a five-year absence.

Remember to allow your students time before engaging in the role playing to think about the situation and about the roles they will play. Keep the role playing to a five-minute period so that the students do not lose interest. Have two children act as reporters to write a brief news story of each event. Allow the performers to react first to their own performances and then have the reporters and the rest of the class react.

Still another teaching tool to use here to motivate students to think about the future is *word association*. Remember that unlike brainstorming, word association calls for rapid-fire responses of one, two, or, at most, three words. Write the responses on the board as the students call them out (or, again, have a student act as secretary). You are not asking for volunteers here. Work around the room calling for a response to each word from each student:

future	tomorrow	yesterday	graduation
hopes	expectations	dreams	2084
goals	growing up	marriage	parenthood
college	career	Judaism	travel

A short writing experience could follow any one of these activities:

1. "The decision I regret having made."
2. "The decision I regret *not* having made."
3. "My wish for the future."
4. "What I want to be most/least remembered for."
5. "Where I want to live/what I want to do in the future."
6. "What scares me about the future."
7. "What being Jewish means to me."
8. "An *authentic* Jew is one who."
9. "The Jew I want my grandchildren to be."

Suggested Classroom and Homework Activities

1. Design your own coat of arms. (See duplicating master #25.)

A coat of arms was a garment worn over medieval armor often embroidered with heraldic or royal symbols representing the reigning monarch of the wearer. (Heraldry is also defined as the art of tracing and recording genealogies.)

Most Jewish families do not have a family coat of arms. These were mainly issued by the monarch to noble families within the non-Jewish community. It was rare for a Jewish family to obtain such a seal. One famous exception is the Rothschild family, whose name itself indicated a family coat of arms. The name Rothschild actually means "red shield."

Create a coat of arms for your family. Think about yourself and your direct ancestors (parents, grandparents). Draw a picture, a design, or a symbol that represents members of your family. The representation may be a personal characteristic of an occupation. Your completed work will become your own family coat of arms.

2. Read the following statement by Maimonides and ask each student to write his or her own statement on *free will.*

   Do not imagine that character is determined at birth. We have been given free will. Any person can become as righteous as Moses or as wicked as Jereboam. We ourselves decide whether to make ourselves learned or ignorant, compassionate or cruel, generous or miserly. No one forces us, no one decides for us, no one drags us along one path or the other; we ourselves, by our own volition, choose our own way.

3. Have your students plan family reunions, on a small, inexpensive scale at first, with everyone bringing a favorite dish to share. Students can invite aunts, uncles, cousins.

4. There are numerous genealogies in the Bible, for example:

   Adam (Gen. 5:1–32)
   Noah's sons Shem, Ham, Japeth (Gen. 10:1–32)
   Abraham's father Terah (Gen. 11:27–12:9)
   Abraham and Hagar's son Ishmael (Gen. 25:2–18)
   Isaac's son Esau (Gen. 36:1–43)
   Jacob's sons (Gen. 46:8–27)

These genealogies teach us that because we are descended from one God we are all *one*; there is a *unity* to all of humankind and this *unity* gives us strength as a people. After reading these genealogies, ask your students to write their own family genealogy in the Biblical style. The family tree and direct ancestry line are other ways for family history information to be recorded.

It would be appropriate to conclude this guide with comments from Arthur Kurzweil.

"You have had the opportunity with this guide to help your students gather a great deal of information about themselves and their family. Hopefully, you have used the guide, as well. Your students will have the opportunity in their lifetime to make many choices and decisions. I hope what they have learned here will help them.
In the Talmud, it is recorded:"

The masters of Yavneh were in the habit of saying:
"I am a creature and my fellow man is a creature.
My work is in the city and his work is in the field.
I rise early to go to my work, and he rises early to go
to his work. As he does not pride himself on his work,
so I do not pride myself on mine.
But should you think that I am doing more than he—
we have learned:
'Do more, do less, it matters not,
so long as one's heart is turned to heaven.'"

Ber. 17a

Chapter 10 at a glance:

Duplicating Master:

1. Family Coat of Arms (#25)

GENEALOGIST'S BOOKSHELF

A Basic Bibliography for Your School or Synagogue Library

To help your students pursue their Jewish family histories, you should familiarize them with some basic "tools." The following bibliography comprises a core collection of items of great use to the Jewish genealogist.

Ask your school or synagogue librarian to check if these items are in the library collection. You might suggest they be placed on a special shelf near the *Encyclopedia Judaica* so your students will always know where the genealogy books are located.

Beard, Timothy Field. *How To Find Your Family Roots*. New York: McGraw-Hill Book Co., 1977.

Cohen, Chester G. *The Shtetl Finder*. Los Angeles: Periday,1980 (Box 583, Woodland Hills, Ca. 91365).

The Columbia Lippincott Gazetteer of the World, with 1961 Supplement. New York: Columbia University Press, 1952 ($175).

Dobroszycki, Lucjan. *Image Before My Eyes: A Photographic History of Jewish Life in Poland, 1864–1939*. New York: Schocken Books, 1977.

Kagan, Berl. *Hebrew Subscription Lists with an Index to 8,767 Jewish Communities in Europe and North Africa*. New York: KTAV, 1975.

Kaganoff, Benzion. *A Dictionary of Jewish Names and Their History*. New York: Schocken Books, 1977.

Kranzler, David. *My Jewish Roots*. New York: Sepher-Hermon Press, 1979.

Kurzweil, Arthur. *From Generation to Generation: How To Trace Your Jewish Genealogy and Personal History*. New York: William Morrow and Co., 1980.

Lifton, Betty Jean. *Lost and Found: The Adoption Experience*. New York: Doubleday & Co., 1979.

Postal, Bernard. *Traveler's Guide to Jewish Landmarks of Europe*. New York: Fleet Press, 1971. (160 Fifth Avenue, New York 10010). Fleet also published the American Jewish Landmark Series by Postal and Lionel Koppman: vol. 1, *The East*, vol.2, *The South and the Southwest*, vol. 3, *The Middle West and the West*.

Rosenstein, Neil. *The Unbroken Chain*. New York: Shengold, 1976.

Rottenberg, Dan. *Finding Our Fathers: A Guidebook to Jewish Genealogy*. New York: Random House, 1977.

Schepansky, Israel. *Holocaust Calendar of Polish Jewry* (2220 Avenue L, Brooklyn, New York 11210).

Stern, Malcolm. *First American Jewish Families: 600 Genealogies 1654–1977*. Cincinnati: American Jewish Archives, 1978.

Toledot: The Journal of Jewish Genealogy (155 East 93rd Street, Suite 3C, New York 10028).

NAME ____________________________

A MAP OF MY NEIGHBORHOOD

On page 9 in *My Generations*, there is space for you to draw a map of your neighborhood. Before drawing your map, take a tour of your neighborhood and list the places you want to include. Sketch some of the important buildings and intersections. *Don't forget to take a camera with you*! (see pages 12–13). You may want to include: your house, synagogue(s), rabbi's house, library, schools, parks, hospital, friends' houses, Y or Jewish Community Center.

NAME ______________________________

A MAP OF MY NEIGHBORHOOD

On page 9 in *My Generations*, there is space for you to draw a map of your neighborhood. Before drawing your map, take a tour of your neighborhood and list the places you want to include. Sketch some of the important buildings and intersections. Don't forget to take a camera with you! (see pages 12–13). You may want to include: your house, synagogue(s), rabbi's house, library, schools, parks, hospital, friends' houses, Y or Jewish Community Center.

 NAME ______________________________

GUIDE TO SOURCES FOR FURTHER RESEARCH

Genealogy and family history, like stamp collecting, can become a lifelong hobby. Here are some sources you can use to continue your search:

1. If you know the name of the steamship an ancestor sailed on and the date of arrival in America, the National Archives will check its collection of passenger lists. To obtain a copy of a passenger list, a form must be completed. Write:

   National Archives and Records Service
   General Services Administration (GSA)
   Washington, D.C. 20408

   In Canada, write:

   Archives Branch
   Public Archives of Canada
   395 Wellington Street
   Ottawa, Ontario K1A ON3

2. Photographs of the steamships immigrant ancestors sailed on are also available from several sources. For information, write to:

   The Mariner's Museum
   Newport News, VA 23606

   Steamship Historical Photo Bank
   University of Baltimore Library
   1420 Maryland Avenue
   Baltimore, MD 21201

3. Birth, death, and marriage records in the United States are available. The best guides to these records can be found in a series of government pamphlets. Write to:

   U.S. Government Printing Office
   Washington, D.C. 20402

4. There are many local Jewish historical societies. Most of them hold regular meetings and publish historical materials. If you live in the vicinity of any of them, you may want to join. To find out if a Jewish historical society exists in your area, write to:

   American Jewish Historical Society
   2 Thornton Rd.
   Waltham, MA 02154

5. Valuable collections of historical materials are kept in archives and are available to genealogists. You may want to write to or visit one of these archival institutions. In addition to those in the following list, there are synagogues that keep their own records.

   American Jewish Archives
   3101 Clifton Avenue
   Cincinnati, Ohio 45220

   Yivo Institute for Jewish Research
   1048 Fifth Avenue
   New York, New York 10028

   Leo Baeck Institute
   129 East 73rd Street
   New York, New York 10021

6. The best guidebook to Jewish genealogical research is *From Generation To Generation: How to Trace Your Jewish Genealogy and Personal History* (Schocken paperback). It was written by Arthur Kurzweil, author of *My Generations*, and contains everything you need to know to become an expert family historian.

NAME ______________________

GUIDE TO SOURCES FOR FURTHER RESEARCH

Genealogy and family history, like stamp collecting, can become a lifelong hobby. Here are some sources you can use to continue your search:

1. If you know the name of the steamship an ancestor sailed on and the date of arrival in America, the National Archives will check its collection of passenger lists. To obtain a copy of a passenger list, a form must be completed. Write:

   National Archives and Records Service
   General Services Administration (GSA)
   Washington, D.C. 20408

   In Canada, write:

   Archives Branch
   Public Archives of Canada
   395 Wellington Street
   Ottawa, Ontario K1A 0N3

2. Photographs of the steamships immigrant ancestors sailed on are also available from several sources. For information, write to:

   The Mariner's Museum
   Newport News, VA 23606

   Steamship Historical Photo Bank
   University of Baltimore Library
   1420 Maryland Avenue
   Baltimore, MD 21201

3. Birth, death, and marriage records in the United States are available. The best guides to these records can be found in a series of government pamphlets. Write to:

   U.S. Government Printing Office
   Washington, D.C. 20402

4. There are many local Jewish historical societies. Most of them hold regular meetings and publish historical materials. If you live in the vicinity of any of them, you may want to join. To find out if a Jewish historical society exists in your area, write to:

   American Jewish Historical Society
   2 Thornton Rd.
   Waltham, MA 02154

5. Valuable collections of historical materials are kept in archives and are available to genealogists. You may want to write to or visit one of these archival institutions. In addition to those in the following list, there are synagogues that keep their own records.

   American Jewish Archives
   3101 Clifton Avenue
   Cincinnati, Ohio 45220

   Yivo Institute for Jewish Research
   1048 Fifth Avenue
   New York, New York 10028

   Leo Baeck Institute
   129 East 73rd Street
   New York, New York 10021

6. The best guidebook to Jewish genealogical research is *From Generation To Generation: How to Trace Your Jewish Genealogy and Personal History* (Schocken paperback). It was written by Arthur Kurzweil, author of *My Generations*, and contains everything you need to know to become an expert family historian.

GUIDE TO SOURCES FOR FURTHER RESEARCH

 NAME ______________________

FAMOUS JEWISH MOVES AND MINE

On page 7, in *My Generations*, Arthur Kurzweil writes: "One could say that history is, in part, the story of people and families moving from one place to another." Here are some famous "moves" in Jewish history. Fill in the blanks with the proper locations for each of these important Jewish moves.

1. Adam and Eve moved out of ______________________. They were expelled by God after disobeying His command not to eat of the Tree of Knowledge.
2. In about 2000 B.C.E., Abraham and Sarah moved from ______________________ to Canaan, the Promised Land, on God's command to leave the city of idol-worshippers and start a new religion.
3. Moses led the escape of the Israelites from ______________________ to Canaan in about 1200 B.C.E. Moses' anger at God prevented him from entering the Promised Land with his people.
4. The armies of Babylonia, led by Nebuchadnezzar, captured and destroyed Jerusalem and Solomon's Temple in 586 B.C.E. The Hebrews were sent from Judah into exile in ______________________.
5. In 1492 Jews were forced to leave ______________________ on the order of Queen Isabella and King Ferdinand. Some fled to Portugal but were also expelled. Those who chose to live secretly as Jews were called Marranos.
6. Jewish refugees from Recife, Brazil arrived in ______________________ in 1654 C.E. These twenty-three Jews were descendants of those expelled from Spain 150 years earlier.
7. Between 1840 and 1860 more than 225,000 ______________________ Jews moved to America to flee religious persecution and oppression. Large department stores such as Gimbel's, Abraham and Straus, Macy's, and Sears, Roebuck were founded by these immigrants.
8. In 1881, after the death of Czar Alexander II, organized riots— *pogroms*— against Jewish communities forced thousands of Jews to move from large cities like Moscow to smaller towns. Many left ______________________ for other countries in Europe and for America and Palestine.
9. Between 1933 and 1945 when Hitler ruled ______________________, Jews in Eastern Europe were forced to leave home. Six million never returned.
10. On May 14, 1948, the State of ______________________ was born. Nearly 700,000 Jews moved to Israel during the first three years of its Statehood. They came from Eastern Europe and Arab countries such as Iraq, Iran, Yemen, Libya, and Morocco.

My Own Family's Moves
(describe your family's last move).

____

____

____

____

____

NAME ______________________________

FAMOUS JEWISH MOVES AND MINE

On page 7, in *My Generations*, Arthur Kurzweil writes: "One could say that history is, in part, the story of people and families moving from one place to another." Here are some famous "moves" in Jewish history. Fill in the blanks with the proper locations for each of these important Jewish moves.

1. Adam and Eve moved out of ______________. They were expelled by God after disobeying His command not to eat of the Tree of Knowledge.

2. In about 2000 B.C.E., Abraham and Sarah moved from ______________ to Canaan, the Promised Land, on God's command to leave the city of idol-worshippers and start a new religion.

3. Moses led the escape of the Israelites from ______________ to Canaan in about 1200 B.C.E. Moses' anger at God prevented him from entering the Promised Land with his people.

4. The armies of Babylonia, led by Nebuchadnezzar, captured and destroyed Jerusalem and Solomon's Temple in 586 B.C.E. The Hebrews were sent from Judah into exile in ______________.

5. In 1492 Jews were forced to leave ______________ on the order of Queen Isabella and King Ferdinand. Some fled to Portugal but were also expelled. Those who chose to live secretly as Jews were called Marranos.

6. Jewish refugees from Recife, Brazil arrived in ______________ in 1654 C.E. These twenty-three Jews were descendants of those expelled from Spain 150 years earlier.

7. Between 1840 and 1860 more than 225,000 ______________ Jews moved to America to flee religious persecution and oppression. Large department stores such as Gimbel's, Abraham and Straus, Macy's, and Sears, Roebuck were founded by these immigrants.

8. In 1881, after the death of Czar Alexander II, organized riots—pogroms—against Jewish communities forced thousands of Jews to move from large cities like Moscow to smaller towns. Many left ______________ for other countries in Europe and for America and Palestine.

9. Between 1933 and 1945 when Hitler ruled ______________, Jews in Eastern Europe were forced to leave home. Six million never returned.

10. On May 14, 1948, the State of ______________ was born. Nearly 700,000 Jews moved to Israel during the first three years of its Statehood. They came from Eastern Europe and Arab countries such as Iraq, Iran, Yemen, Libya, and Morocco.

My Own Family's Moves
(describe your family's last move).

____

____

____

____

____

 NAME ____________________

HOW ARE WE RELATED?

Relationship Chart

	0	1	2	3	4	5	6
0	CP	S	GS	GGS	2 GGS	3 GGS	4 GGS
1	S	B	N	GN	GGN	2 GGN	3 GGN
2	GS	N	1C	1C 1R	1C 2R	1C 3R	1C 4R
3	GGS	GN	1C 1R	2C	2C 1R	2C 2R	2C 3R
4	2 GGS	GGN	1C 2R	2C 1R	3C	3C 1R	3C 2R
5	3 GGS	2 GGN	1C 3R	2C 2R	3C 1R	4C	4C 1R
6	4 GGS	3 GGN	1C 4R	2C 3R	3C 2R	4C 1R	5C

CP = Common Progenitor
C = Cousin
B = Brother or Sister
R = Times Removed
S = Son or Daughter
N = Nephew or Niece
GS = Grandson or Granddaughter
GGS = Great-grandson or Great granddaughter

How are you related to:

- Your father's first cousin?
- Your mother's first cousin's son?
- Your mother's sister's son?
- Your paternal grandfather's sister's daughter?
- Your maternal grandmother's first cousin?

Write in pencil so you can use the chart many times. *Good luck!*

NAME ______________________________________

HOW ARE WE RELATED?

Relationship Chart

	0	1	2	3	4	5	6
0	CP	S	GS	GGS	2 GGS	3 GGS	4 GGS
1	S	B	N	GN	GGN	2 GGN	3 GGN
2	GS	N	1C	1C 1R	1C 2R	1C 3R	1C 4R
3	GGS	GN	1C 1R	2C	2C 1R	2C 2R	2C 3R
4	2 GGS	GGN	1C 2R	2C 1R	3C	3C 1R	3C 2R
5	3 GGS	2 GGN	1C 3R	2C 2R	3C 1R	4C	4C 1R
6	4 GGS	3 GGN	1C 4R	2C 3R	3C 2R	4C 1R	5C

CP = Common Progenitor
C = Cousin
B = Brother or Sister
R = Times Removed
S = Son or Daughter

N = Nephew or Niece
GS = Grandson or Granddaughter
GGS = Great-grandson or Great granddaughter

How are you related to:

Your father's first cousin?
Your mother's first cousin's son?
Your mother's sister's son?
Your paternal grandfather's sister's daughter?
Your maternal grandmother's first cousin?

Write in pencil so you can use the chart many times. Good luck!

 NAME ____________________

YIDDISH IS MORE THAN A LANGUAGE

Yiddish was the language of everyday life in the shtetl. The language uses the Hebrew alphabet but evolved out of the German language heard by Jewish settlers in northern France about 1000 years ago. As Jews settled throughout Germany, they added words from other languages. Yiddish is a language which is three-fourths German and the rest a mixture of Hebrew, Polish, Russian, and Rumanian. Many Yiddish words have entered the English vocabulary as you can see below.

BAGEL—a hard doughnut-shaped roll
BALABATISH—quiet, respectable, well-mannered
BORSCHT—beet soup, served hot or cold
CHEDER—school
CHUTZPA—nerve; presumption
DAVEN—to pray
FEH!—phooey
GELT—money
GANEF—thief
KIBBITZ—to joke around
KLUTZ—a clumsy person
MAVIN—an expert
MELAMED—teacher
MENCH—an upright, honorable person
MESHUGGE—crazy
NACHUS—proud pleasure
NOSH—snack
NUDNIK—pest; nag
SCHMALTZ—chicken fat
SCHNEIDER—tailor
SCHNORRER—beggar
SCHATCHEN—a professional matchmaker
SHAMMES—the caretaker of a synagogue
SHUL—synagogue
TRAYF—any food that is not kosher
YENTA—a gossipy woman
YICHES—family status or prestige

How well do you understand these Yiddish words? Fill in the missing Yiddish word here.

Don't buy it until you get the advice of a ____________________.

Traditional Jews ____________________ three times a day.

You don't need teeth to eat ____________________.

If you smell a rotten egg, say ____________________.

The highest ____________________ attaches to the man of learning.

A ____________________ is known as a doughnut with a college education.

The finest thing you can say about a man is that he is a ____________________.

"If I were Rockefeller," said the ____________________, "I'd be richer than Rockefeller because I'd do a little teaching on the side."

Parents get ____________________ from their children.

Do you think you could write a story using some Yiddish words? Try it and *zay gezunt!*

____

____

____

____

____

NAME ______________________

YIDDISH IS MORE THAN A LANGUAGE

Yiddish was the language of everyday life in the shtetl. The language uses the Hebrew alphabet but evolved out of the German language heard by Jewish settlers in northern France about 1000 years ago. As Jews settled throughout Germany, they added words from other languages. Yiddish is a language which is three-fourths German and the rest a mixture of Hebrew, Polish, Russian, and Rumanian. Many Yiddish words have entered the English vocabulary as you can see below.

BAGEL—a hard doughnut-shaped roll
BALABATISH—quiet, respectable, well-mannered
BORSCHT—beet soup, served hot or cold
CHEDER—school
CHUTZPA—nerve; presumption
DAVEN—to pray
FEHI—phooey
GELT—money
GANEF—thief
KIBBITZ—to joke around
KLUTZ—a clumsy person
MAVIN—an expert
MELAMED—teacher

MENCH—an upright, honorable person
MESHUGGE—crazy
NACHUS—proud pleasure
NOSH—snack
NUDNIK—pest; nag
SCHMALTZ—chicken fat
SCHNEIDER—tailor
SCHNORRER—beggar
SCHATCHEN—a professional matchmaker
SHAMMES—the caretaker of a synagogue
SHUL—synagogue
TRAYF—any food that is not kosher
YENTA—a gossipy woman
YICHES—family status or prestige

How well do you understand these Yiddish words? Fill in the missing Yiddish word here.

Don't buy it until you get the advice of a ______________________.

Traditional Jews ______________ three times a day.

You don't need teeth to eat ______________________.

If you smell a rotten egg, say ______________________.

The highest ______________ attaches to the man of learning.

A ______________ is known as a doughnut with a college education.

The finest thing you can say about a man is that he is a ______________________.

"If I were Rockefeller," said the ______________, "I'd be richer than Rockefeller because I'd do a little teaching on the side."

Parents get ______________ from their children.

Do you think you could write a story using some Yiddish words? Try it and zay gezunt!

____

____

____

____

____

MASTER #5 NAME ____________________

YIDDISH IS MORE THAN A LANGUAGE

MASTER #6

NAME ____________________

ADDITIONAL GENEALOGICAL DATA

NAME ____________________
BORN ____________________
DATE PLACE
MARRIED ____________________
DATE PLACE
DIED ____________________
DATE PLACE

NAME ____________________
BORN ____________________
DATE PLACE
MARRIED ____________________
DATE PLACE
DIED ____________________
DATE PLACE

NAME ____________________
BORN ____________________
DATE PLACE
MARRIED ____________________
DATE PLACE
DIED ____________________
DATE PLACE

NAME ____________________
BORN ____________________
DATE PLACE
MARRIED ____________________
DATE PLACE
DIED ____________________
DATE PLACE

NAME ____________________
BORN ____________________
DATE PLACE
MARRIED ____________________
DATE PLACE
DIED ____________________
DATE PLACE

NAME ____________________
BORN ____________________
DATE PLACE
MARRIED ____________________
DATE PLACE
DIED ____________________
DATE PLACE

NAME ____________________
BORN ____________________
DATE PLACE
MARRIED ____________________
DATE PLACE
DIED ____________________
DATE PLACE

NAME ____________________
BORN ____________________
DATE PLACE
MARRIED ____________________
DATE PLACE
DIED ____________________
DATE PLACE

NAME ____________________
BORN ____________________
DATE PLACE
MARRIED ____________________
DATE PLACE
DIED ____________________
DATE PLACE

NAME ____________________
BORN ____________________
DATE PLACE
MARRIED ____________________
DATE PLACE
DIED ____________________
DATE PLACE

NAME ______________________

ADDITIONAL GENEALOGICAL DATA

NAME ______________________
BORN ______________________
DATE PLACE
MARRIED ______________________
DATE PLACE
DIED ______________________
DATE PLACE

NAME ______________________
BORN ______________________
DATE PLACE
MARRIED ______________________
DATE PLACE
DIED ______________________
DATE PLACE

NAME ______________________
BORN ______________________
DATE PLACE
MARRIED ______________________
DATE PLACE
DIED ______________________
DATE PLACE

NAME ______________________
BORN ______________________
DATE PLACE
MARRIED ______________________
DATE PLACE
DIED ______________________
DATE PLACE

NAME ______________________
BORN ______________________
DATE PLACE
MARRIED ______________________
DATE PLACE
DIED ______________________
DATE PLACE

NAME ______________________
BORN ______________________
DATE PLACE
MARRIED ______________________
DATE PLACE
DIED ______________________
DATE PLACE

NAME ______________________
BORN ______________________
DATE PLACE
MARRIED ______________________
DATE PLACE
DIED ______________________
DATE PLACE

NAME ______________________
BORN ______________________
DATE PLACE
MARRIED ______________________
DATE PLACE
DIED ______________________
DATE PLACE

NAME ______________________
BORN ______________________
DATE PLACE
MARRIED ______________________
DATE PLACE
DIED ______________________
DATE PLACE

NAME ______________________
BORN ______________________
DATE PLACE
MARRIED ______________________
DATE PLACE
DIED ______________________
DATE PLACE

 NAME ______________________________

NAMES IN THE TORAH

In the first chapter of the Torah, Genesis, God names five things. What are they?

____

____

____

____

____

God also changed some names. *Avrum* became *Abraham*; *Sarai*, his wife, became *Sarah*. In the Bible, there are several other name changes. Can you find them?

Jacob becomes ______________________________

Why was his name changed? ______________________________

____

Gideon becomes ______________________________

Why was his name changed? ______________________________

____

Hoshea becomes ______________________________

Why was his name changed? ______________________________

____

Have there been name changes in your family? Why?

____

____

NAME ______________________________

NAMES IN THE TORAH

In the first chapter of the Torah, Genesis, God names five things. What are they?

____

____

____

____

____

God also changed some names. Avrum became Abraham; Sarai, his wife, became Sarah. In the Bible, there are several other name changes. Can you find them?

Jacob becomes ______________________________

Why was his name changed? ______________________________

____

Gideon becomes ______________________________

Why was his name changed? ______________________________

____

Hoshea becomes ______________________________

Why was his name changed? ______________________________

____

Have there been name changes in your family? Why?

____

____

MASTER #8 NAME ____________________

FAMOUS JEWS WHO HAVE CHANGED THEIR NAMES

Can you match the present and former names of Jews who have changed names?

Present	Former
1. Woody Allen	A) Melvin Kaminsky
2. Lauren Bacall	B) Howard Cohen
3. Mel Brooks	C) Bernard Schwartz
4. Howard Cosell	D) Allen Konigsberg
5. Tony Curtis	E) Irwin Kniberg
6. Elliot Gould	F) Leonard Rosenberg
7. Bob Dylan	G) Belle Silverman
8. Mike Wallace	H) Robert Zimmerman
9. Beverly Sills	I) Betty Joan Perske
10. Dick Shawn	J) Elliot Goldstein
11. Joan Rivers	K) Mike Wallach
12. Tony Randall	L) Richard Schulef
13. Jerry Lewis	M) Joseph Levitch
14. Alan King	N) Joan Molinsky
15. Dr. Joyce Brothers	O) Melvin Israel
16. Kirk Douglas	P) Eugene Silverstein
17. Lee Grant	Q) Milton Hines
18. Danny Kaye	R) Benjamin Kubelsky
19. Jack Benny	S) Daniel Kaminsky
20. Tony Martin	T) Lyova Rosenthal
21. Mike Nichols	U) Leonard Hacker
22. Soupy Sales	V) Joyce Bauer
23. Gene Wilder	W) Issur Danilovich Demsky
24. Buddy Hackett	X) Alvin Morris
25. Mel Allen	Y) Michael Igor Peschlowsky
26. Dinah Shore	Z) Francis Rose Shore

NAME ____________________

FAMOUS JEWS WHO HAVE CHANGED THEIR NAMES

Can you match the present and former names of Jews who have changed names?

Present	Former
1. Woody Allen	A) Melvin Kaminsky
2. Lauren Bacall	B) Howard Cohen
3. Mel Brooks	C) Bernard Schwartz
4. Howard Cosell	D) Allen Konigsberg
5. Tony Curtis	E) Irwin Kniberg
6. Elliot Gould	F) Leonard Rosenberg
7. Bob Dylan	G) Belle Silverman
8. Mike Wallace	H) Robert Zimmerman
9. Beverly Sills	I) Betty Joan Perske
10. Dick Shawn	J) Elliot Goldstein
11. Joan Rivers	K) Mike Wallach
12. Tony Randall	L) Richard Schulef
13. Jerry Lewis	M) Joseph Levitch
14. Alan King	N) Joan Molinsky
15. Dr. Joyce Brothers	O) Melvin Israel
16. Kirk Douglas	P) Eugene Silverstein
17. Lee Grant	Q) Milton Hines
18. Danny Kaye	R) Benjamin Kubelsky
19. Jack Benny	S) Daniel Kaminsky
20. Tony Martin	T) Lyova Rosenthal
21. Mike Nichols	U) Leonard Hacker
22. Soupy Sales	V) Joyce Bauer
23. Gene Wilder	W) Issur Danilovich Demsky
24. Buddy Hackett	X) Alvin Morris
25. Mel Allen	Y) Michael Igor Peschlowsky
26. Dinah Shore	Z) Francis Rose Shore

NAME ______________________________

FAMOUS JEWS WHO HAVE CHANGED THEIR NAMES

MASTER #9 NAME ____________________

FAMOUS SIGNATURES

As you know, the name of a person written in his or her own hand is called a signature. People have distinct signatures. Here is Arthur Kurzweil's

What does yours look like? ____________________

Here are some signatures of famous Jews to examine. Can you figure out whose signatures they are? The list of names at the bottom will help.

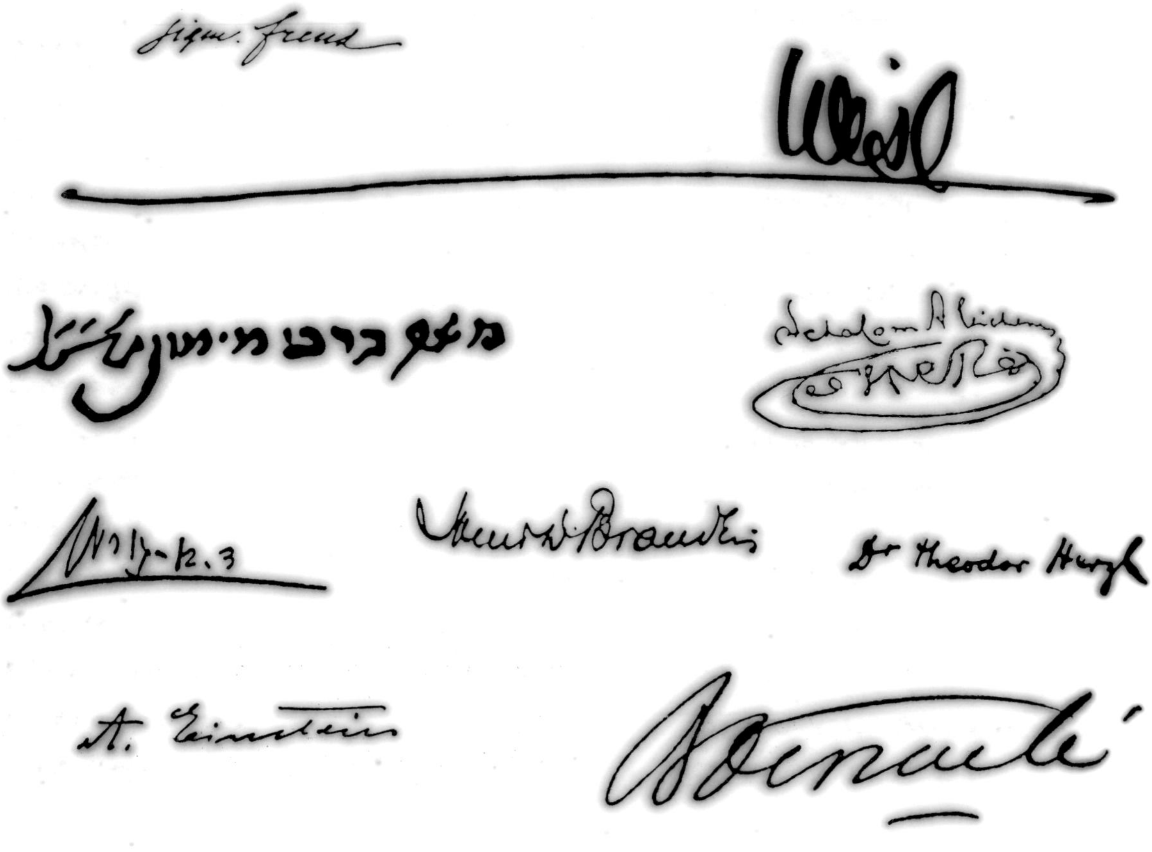

Theodor Herzl	Shalom Aleichem	Stephen S. Wise
Maimonides	David Ben-Gurion	Sigmund Freud
Louis D. Brandeis	Albert Einstein	Benjamin Disraeli

NAME ______________________________

FAMOUS SIGNATURES

As you know, the name of a person written in his or her own hand is called a signature. People have distinct signatures. Here is Arthur Kurzweil's

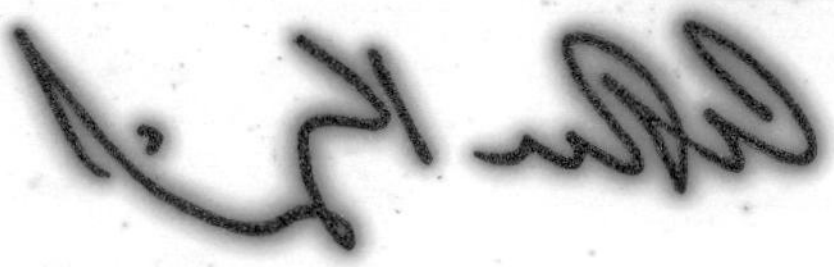

What does yours look like? ______________________________

Here are some signatures of famous Jews to examine. Can you figure out whose signatures they are? The list of names at the bottom will help.

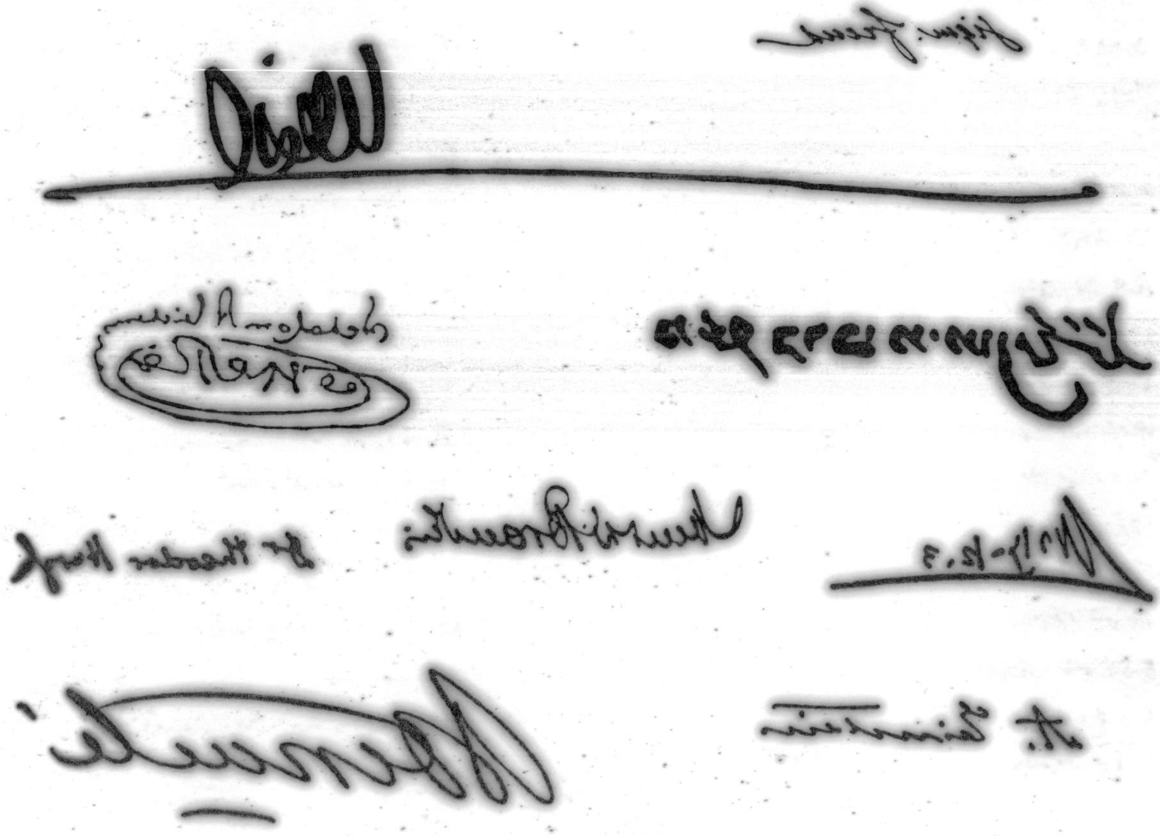

Theodor Herzl	Shalom Aleichem	Stephen S. Wise
Maimonides	David Ben-Gurion	Sigmund Freud
Louis D. Brandeis	Albert Einstein	Benjamin Disraeli

MASTER [illegible]   NAME ________________________

[illegible]

 NAME ______________________

WHAT'S IN A NAME? MORE THAN YOU THINK

Here is a list of selected Jewish names derived from occupations. Do you know the origin of your family name?

ABZUG—printer
ACKERMAN—plowman
ANTMAN—handyman
BALSAM—pharmacist
BASS—singer
BECKMAN—baker
BENDER—cask maker
BESSER—tax collector or rabbinic judge
BICKEL—handyman
BINDER—bookbinder
BLASER—shofar blower
BLECHER—tinsmith
BODNER—barrel maker
BOTNICK—ladies shoe manufacturer
BRAND—distiller
BRANDER, BRENDER—distiller
BRAVERMAN—brewer
BREYER—brewer
BRILLIANT—dealer in precious stones
BROITMAN—baker
BRONFMAN—whiskey seller
BULKA—baker
BUXBAUM—woodworker
CHAIT—tailor
CHASIN, CHASINS, CHASON—cantor
CHERNIK—seller of sepia
CITRON—lemon seller
DAUBER—pigeon seller
DRUCKER—printer
EDELSTEIN—dealer in precious stones
EINSTEIN—mason
FEDER—scribe
FEDERBUSCH—dealer in feathers
FEINBERG—wine seller
FEINER—wine producer
FEINGOLD, FEINSILVER—dealer in gold or silver
FEINSTEIN—jeweler
FELLER—trader in hides
FENSTER—producer of windows and doors
FINE—wine merchant
FINK—dealer in precious gems
FLAXMAN—dealer in flax
FLEISHMAN—butcher
FLEISCHER—butcher
FORMAN—teamster
FUTTERMAN—furrier
GALINSKY—grain seller
GARBER—tanner
GARFUNKEL—diamond dealer
GEFFEN—wine merchant
GEIGER—violinist
GITTELMAN—cap maker
GLASS—glassmaker
GOLDSCHEIDER—goldsmith
GOLDSCHMIDT—goldsmith
GOLDSTEIN—goldsmith
GRABER—engraver
GREENSPAN—paint seller
GUTMACHER—hat maker
HABER—judge
HASPEL—dealer in yarn
HOFFMAN—farmer
HOLZMAN—timber trader
HUBERMAN—oat dealer
KADAR—barrel maker
KAUFMAN—merchant
KAZAN—cantor
KIMMELMAN—grocer
KIRZNER—furrier
KLASS—entertainer
KLEPFISH—merchant
KLINGER—junk dealer
KOLATCH—baker
KOLODNY—cask or barrel maker
KORF, KORFF—basket maker
KORN—grain dealer
KORSHAK—tavern owner
KRATCHMER—innkeeper
KRENSKY—seller of bleach
KROCHMAL—dealer in starch
KRUPNICK—manufacturer of groats
KUSHNER—furrier
LAFFER—traveling furrier
LAPIDUS—gem engraver
LEDERER—dyer of leather
LEHMAN—banker
LERNER—student
LICHTERMAN—tax collector
LICHTZER—candle dipper
LOPATA—baker
LOTSTEIN—glazier
MAGIDSON—preacher
MAHLER—miller
MARANS—dealer in oranges
MARMELSTEIN—builder
MASS—bookseller
MAUTNER—toll collector
MECKLER—broker
MEHLER—charcoal burner
MEHLMAN—flour merchant
MELNICK—miller
MELZNER—brewer
MESSINGER—dealer in brass
MILLER—miller
MILLMAN—miller
MILSTEIN—miller
MUCHNIK—flour merchant
NAGER—carpenter
NAIMAN—supervisor of religious matters
NASATIR—banker
NERENBERG—merchant
NETZKY—baker
PACKER—peddler
PAPERNICK—paper seller
PASTERNACK—dealer in vegetables
PERGAMENT—scribe
PERLMUTTER—dealer in mother of pearl
PLOTKIN—fish dealer
PLOTNICK—carpenter
PORTNOY—tailor
POTASHNIK—potash maker
PRESSER—tailor who irons clothes
RAUCHWERKER—furrier
REITER—dealer in lumber
RIBALOW—fish dealer
RINGLE—goldsmith
ROBACK—laborer
ROSTHOLDER—dealer in horses
RYMER—harness maker
SALZMAN—seller of salt
SAPERSTEIN—jeweler
SAPOZNIK—shoemaker
SATZ—cantor
SCHACHTEL—ritual slaughterer
SCHAFFNER—manager of a business
SCHARFSTEIN—butcher
SCHINDLER—shingler
SCHLOSS—locksmith
SCHLOSSMAN—locksmith
SCHRIFT—printer
SCHUPACK—fish dealer
SELTZER—salt merchant
SHAFRAN—merchant
SHAMES—sexton
SHERER—barber
SHERMAN—dealer in woolen cloth
SILBERMAN—trader in silver
SILVERSTEIN—jeweler
SKLAR—glazier
SKORA—leather dealer
SMOLER—burner of tar
SOLARZ—salt merchant
SOLODAR—goldsmith
SPECTOR—tutor
SPIEGLER—mirror maker
SPIVAK—cantor
STEINER—jeweler
STEUER—tax collector
STICKER—braider
STOLLER—carpenter
TABACHNIK—seller or manufacturer of snuff
TAMBOR—drummer
TARLER—seller of hardware
TAXIN—tax collector
TEIG—baker
TELLER—barber/surgeon
TENDLER—dealer in secondhand clothes
TESSLER—carpenter
TRUBNICK—butcher or carpenter
TUCHMAN—cloth merchant
TYGEL—goldsmith
WAGNER—cartwright
WALKER—fuller of woolen cloth
WARNIK—operator of salt works
WASSERMAN—water carrier
WAXMAN—wax dealer
WECKER—baker
WEIN—wine merchant
WEINER—wine dealer
WEINGLASS—owner of a wine shop
WEINSTEIN—dealer in wine
WINNICK—distiller
WOLLMAN—trader in wool
ZEGMAN—carpenter
ZEITMAN—watch maker
ZIMBALIST—cymbal player
ZIMMERMAN—carpenter
ZITNICK—grain merchant
ZUCKERMAN—confectioner
ZUNDER—seller of tinder
ZUPNICK—government official
ZWIEBEL—green grocer
ZWIRN—tailor

NAME ______________________

WHAT'S IN A NAME? MORE THAN YOU THINK

Here is a list of selected Jewish names derived from occupations. Do you know the origin of your family name?

ABZUG—printer
ACKERMAN—plowman
ANTMAN—handyman
BALSAM—pharmacist
BASS—singer
BECKMAN—baker
BENDER—cask maker
BESSER—tax collector or rabbinic judge
BICKEL—handyman
BINDER—bookbinder
BLASER—shofar blower
BLECHER—tinsmith
BODNER—barrel maker
BOTNICK—ladies shoe manufacturer
BRAND—distiller
BRANDER, BRENDER—distiller
BRAVERMAN—brewer
BREYER—brewer
BRILLIANT—dealer in precious stones
BROITMAN—baker
BRONFMAN—whiskey seller
BULKA—baker
BUXBAUM—woodworker
CHAIT—tailor
CHASIN, CHASINS, CHASON—cantor
CHERNIK—seller of sepia
CITRON—lemon seller
DAUBER—pigeon seller
DRUCKER—printer
EDELSTEIN—dealer in precious stones
EINSTEIN—mason
FEDER—scribe
FEDERBUSCH—dealer in feathers
FEINBERG—wine seller
FEINER—wine producer
FEINGOLD, FEINSILVER—dealer in gold or silver
FEINSTEIN—jeweler
FELLER—trader in hides
FENSTER—producer of windows and doors
FINE—wine merchant
FINK—dealer in precious gems
FLAXMAN—dealer in flax
FLEISHMAN—butcher
FLEISCHER—butcher
FORMAN—teamster
FUTTERMAN—furrier
GALINSKY—grain seller
GARBER—tanner
GARFUNKEL—diamond dealer
GEFFEN—wine merchant
GEIGER—violinist
GITTELMAN—cap maker
GLASS—glassmaker
GOLDSCHEIDER—goldsmith
GOLDSCHMIDT—goldsmith
GOLDSTEIN—goldsmith
GRABER—engraver
GREENSPAN—paint seller
GUTMACHER—hat maker
HABER—judge
HASPEL—dealer in yarn
HOFFMAN—farmer
HOLZMAN—timber trader
HUBERMAN—oat dealer
KADAR—barrel maker
KAUFMAN—merchant
KAZAN—cantor
KIMMELMAN—grocer
KIRZNER—furrier
KLASS—entertainer
KLEFFISH—merchant
KLINGER—junk dealer
KOLATCH—baker
KOLODNY—cask or barrel maker
KORF, KORFF—basket maker
KORN—grain dealer
KORSHAK—tavern owner
KRATCHMER—innkeeper
KRENSKY—seller of bleach
KROCHMAL—dealer in starch
KRUPNICK—manufacturer of groats
KUSHNER—furrier
LAFFER—traveling furrier
LAPIDUS—gem engraver
LEDERER—dyer of leather
LEHMAN—banker
LERNER—student
LICHTERMAN—tax collector
LICHTZER—candle dipper
LOPATA—baker
LOTSTEIN—glazier
MAGIDSON—preacher
MAHLER—miller
MARANS—dealer in oranges
MARMELSTEIN—builder
MASS—bookseller
MAUTNER—toll collector
MECKLER—broker
MEHLER—charcoal burner
MEHLMAN—flour merchant
MELNICK—miller
MELZNER—brewer
MESSINGER—dealer in brass
MILLER—miller
MILLMAN—miller
MILSTEIN—miller
MUCHNIK—flour merchant
NAGER—carpenter
NAIMAN—supervisor of religious matters
NASATIR—banker
NERENBERG—merchant
NETZKY—baker
PACKER—peddler
PAPERNICK—paper seller
PASTERNACK—dealer in vegetables
PERGAMENT—scribe
PERLMUTTER—dealer in mother of pearl
PLOTKIN—fish dealer
PLOTNICK—carpenter
PORTNOY—tailor
POTASHNIK—potash maker
PRESSER—tailor who irons clothes
RAUCHWERKER—furrier
REITER—dealer in lumber
RIBALOW—fish dealer
RINGLE—goldsmith
ROBACK—laborer
ROSTHOLDER—dealer in horses
RYMER—harness maker
SALZMAN—seller of salt
SAPERSTEIN—jeweler
SAPOZNIK—shoemaker
SATZ—cantor
SCHACHTEL—ritual slaughterer
SCHAFFNER—manager of a business
SCHARFSTEIN—butcher
SCHINDLER—shingler
SCHLOSS—locksmith
SCHLOSSMAN—locksmith
SCHRIFT—printer
SCHUPACK—fish dealer
SELTZER—salt merchant
SHAFRAN—merchant
SHAMES—sexton
SHERER—barber
SHERMAN—dealer in woolen cloth
SILBERMAN—trader in silver
SILVERSTEIN—jeweler
SKLAR—glazier
SKORA—leather dealer
SMOLER—burner of tar
SOLARZ—salt merchant
SOLODAR—goldsmith
SPECTOR—tutor
SPIEGLER—mirror maker
SPIVAK—cantor
STEINER—jeweler
STEUER—tax collector
STICKER—braider
STOLLER—carpenter
TABACHNIK—seller or manufacturer of snuff
TAMBOR—drummer
TARLER—seller of hardware
TAXIN—tax collector
TEIG—baker
TELLER—barber/surgeon
TENDLER—dealer in secondhand clothes
TESSLER—carpenter
TRUBNICK—butcher or carpenter
TUCHMAN—cloth merchant
TYGEL—goldsmith
WAGNER—cartwright
WALKER—fuller of woolen cloth
WARNIK—operator of salt works
WASSERMAN—water carrier
WAXMAN—wax dealer
WECKER—baker
WEIN—wine merchant
WEINER—wine dealer
WEINGLASS—owner of a wine shop
WEINSTEIN—dealer in wine
WINNICK—distiller
WOLLMAN—trader in wool
ZEGMAN—carpenter
ZEITMAN—watch maker
ZIMBALIST—cymbal player
ZIMMERMAN—carpenter
ZITNICK—grain merchant
ZUCKERMAN—confectioner
ZUNDER—seller of tinder
ZUPNICK—government official
ZWIEBEL—green grocer
ZWIRN—tailor

NAME ______________________________

WHAT'S IN A NAME? MORE THAN YOU THINK

A SPECIAL FAMILY RECIPE

My name ______________________ Date ______________

This is a recipe for ______________________________.

The recipe was given to me by ______________________

who learned it from ______________________________.

The recipe was originally prepared in (place of origin) ______________.

The recipe has been in my family for ______________ years.

INGREDIENTS

DIRECTIONS

A special family story connected with this dish: ______________________

____

____

A SPECIAL FAMILY RECIPE

My name ______________________ Date ______________________

This is a recipe for ______________________.

The recipe was given to me by ______________________

who learned it from ______________________.

The recipe was originally prepared in (place of origin) ______________________.

The recipe has been in my family for ______________________ years.

INGREDIENTS

DIRECTIONS

A special family story connected with this dish: ______________________

____

____

A SPECIAL FAMILY RECIPE

 NAME ____________________

FAVORITE HOLIDAY FOODS

We all have holiday foods that are special to us. Can you match the food from the following list with the holiday during which it is eaten?

hamantashen	Shabbat
fruits	Purim
latkes	Passover
honey	Shavuot
matzah	Rosh Hashanah
braided challah	Sukkot
dairy	Hanukkah

1. We eat ____________________ on ____________________ to remind us of the three reasons we celebrate this holiday: to be joyful at the giving of the Ten Commandments; to celebrate the harvesting of wheat in Israel, and to be grateful at the coming of the first fruits.
2. We eat ____________________ on ____________________ to remind us that the Israelites on their way to Canaan, the Promised Land, gathered on Friday, a double portion of *manna* (the food that descended to them from the skies) because on Shabbat, they were not permitted to gather *manna*.
3. We eat ____________________ on ____________________ as we wish for a sweet year.
4. We eat ____________________ on ____________________ as part of our thanksgiving celebration of the harvest and as we wish for a fruitful year to come.
5. We eat ____________________ on ____________________ to remind us of the legend of the oil which burned for 8 days for the Maccabees.
6. We eat ____________________ on ____________________ to remind us of the three-cornered hat that evil Hamon wore.
7. We eat ____________________ on ____________________ to remind us of the bread our ancestors baked hurriedly during their journey to Canaan, the Promised Land.

NAME ____________________________

FAVORITE HOLIDAY FOODS

NAME ____________________

NEW IN THEIR LIFETIME

Who in your family would have been the first to benefit from the invention of:

Invention	Name of family member
1. balloon and parachute (1783)	____________
2. life preserver (1805)	____________
3. bicycle (1816)	____________
4. camera (1822)	____________
5. safety pin (1849)	____________
6. refrigerator and washing machine (1858)	____________
7. linoleum (1860)	____________
8. telephone (1876)	____________
9. phonograph (1877)	____________
10. color photography (1881)	____________
11. motorcycle (1885)	____________
12. automobile (1887)	____________
13. airplane (1903)	____________
14. zipper (1893)	____________
15. electric stove (1896)	____________
16. air conditioner (1911)	____________
17. automatic toaster (1918)	____________
18. television (1926)	____________
19. electric shaver (1928)	____________
20. parking meter (1935)	____________
21. jet engine (1937)	____________
22. aerosol spray (1941)	____________
23. electronic computer (1946)	____________
24. transistor (1948)	____________
25. laser (1960)	____________

What inventions are new in *your* lifetime?

____

____

____

NAME ______________________________

NEW IN THEIR LIFETIME

Who in your family would have been the first to benefit from the invention of:

Invention	Name of family member
1. balloon and parachute (1783)	______________________
2. life preserver (1805)	______________________
3. bicycle (1816)	______________________
4. camera (1822)	______________________
5. safety pin (1849)	______________________
6. refrigerator and washing machine (1858)	______________________
7. linoleum (1860)	______________________
8. telephone (1876)	______________________
9. phonograph (1877)	______________________
10. color photography (1881)	______________________
11. motorcycle (1885)	______________________
12. automobile (1887)	______________________
13. airplane (1903)	______________________
14. zipper (1893)	______________________
15. electric stove (1896)	______________________
16. air conditioner (1911)	______________________
17. automatic toaster (1918)	______________________
18. television (1926)	______________________
19. electric shaver (1928)	______________________
20. parking meter (1935)	______________________
21. jet engine (1937)	______________________
22. aerosol spray (1941)	______________________
23. electronic computer (1946)	______________________
24. transistor (1948)	______________________
25. laser (1960)	______________________

What inventions are new in your lifetime?

____

____

____

NAME ______________________________

NAME ________________________

HOLIDAYS AND THEIR RITUAL OBJECTS

Jewish life is filled with a rich mixture of various kinds of religious and cultural customs, many of which require ritual objects. Some of these may be heirlooms in your family. Just about every Jewish holiday has a unique set of ritual objects to go along with it. What are they?

Next to each of the ritual objects listed below, write the holiday during which it is used. There is space for you to write the names of other ritual objects and customs of that holiday.

1. DREYDEL ________________________

2. GRAGGER ________________________

3. CUP OF ELIJAH ________________________

4. ETROG ________________________

5. KIDDISH CUP ________________________

6. SHOFAR ________________________

7. TORAH ________________________

8. SHAVUOT ________________________

NAME ______________________________

HOLIDAYS AND THEIR RITUAL OBJECTS

Jewish life is filled with a rich mixture of various kinds of religious and cultural customs, many of which require ritual objects. Some of these may be heirlooms in your family. Just about every Jewish holiday has a unique set of ritual objects to go along with it. What are they?

Next to each of the ritual objects listed below, write the holiday during which it is used. There is space for you to write the names of other ritual objects and customs of that holiday.

1. DREYDEL ______________________________

2. GRAGGER ______________________________

3. CUP OF ELIJAH ______________________________

4. ETROG ______________________________

5. KIDDISH CUP ______________________________

6. SHOFAR ______________________________

7. TORAH ______________________________

8. SHAVUOT ______________________________

FAVORITE FAMILY JOKES

FAVORITE FAMILY JOKES

FAVORITE FAMILY JOKES

MASTER #16 NAME ____________________

MY CONGREGATION'S HISTORY

How well do you know the history of your congregation You may want to ask an older member of the congregation some of these questions. Perhaps a member of your family who is a longtime member of the congregation can help you.

First, here are some questions for you to answer.

1. When did you join the ____________________ synagogue?

____

2. Why did you join this particular synagogue?

____

3. What synagogue did you belong to before joining this one?

____

4. Why did you leave that synagogue?

____

5. What do you like best about your synagogue?

____

Now, here are some questions for you to ask others.

1. How old is your synagogue? ____________________
2. Who founded it? ____________________
3. Why was it founded? ____________________
4. What does its name mean? ____________________
5. How many members are in the congregation? ____________________
6. How many students are in the religious school? ____________________
7. Who is the principal? ____________________
8. What is the rabbi's name? ____________________
9. Who was the first rabbi? ____________________
10. What mitzvah projects does the congregation engage in? ____________________

Additional questions to ask:

____

____

____

NAME ______________________________

MY CONGREGATION'S HISTORY

How well do you know the history of your congregation You may want to ask an older member of the congregation some of these questions. Perhaps a member of your family who is a longtime member of the congregation can help you.

First, here are some questions for you to answer.

1. When did you join the ______________________ synagogue?
____

2. Why did you join this particular synagogue?
____

3. What synagogue did you belong to before joining this one?
____

4. Why did you leave that synagogue?
____

5. What do you like best about your synagogue?
____

Now, here are some questions for you to ask others.

1. How old is your synagogue? ______________________
2. Who founded it? ______________________
3. Why was it founded? ______________________
4. What does its name mean? ______________________
5. How many members are in the congregation? ______________________
6. How many students are in the religious school? ______________________
7. Who is the principal? ______________________
8. What is the rabbi's name? ______________________
9. Who was the first rabbi? ______________________
10. What mitzvah projects does the congregation engage in? ______________________

Additional questions to ask:

____

____

____

NAME ____________________

TELL ME, RABBI

How much do you know about what it means to be a rabbi? How well do you know the rabbi of your congregation? Here are some questions you may want answered.

1. What made you decide to become a rabbi? ____________________

2. What kind of training did you need? ____________________

3. What was the name of the seminary you attended? ____________________

4. How did you come to take the pulpit at our synagogue? ____________________

5. What do you need to do to prepare for each service? ____________________

6. Besides leading the congregation in worship, what are your other responsibilities? ____________________

7. What do you like most about being a rabbi? What do you like least? ____________________

Additional questions:

____

NAME ______________________________

TELL ME, RABBI

How much do you know about what it means to be a rabbi? How well do you know the rabbi of your congregation? Here are some questions you may want answered.

1. What made you decide to become a rabbi? ______________________________

2. What kind of training did you need? ______________________________

3. What was the name of the seminary you attended? ______________________________

4. How did you come to take the pulpit at our synagogue? ______________________________

5. What do you need to do to prepare for each service? ______________________________

6. Besides leading the congregation in worship, what are your other responsibilities? ______________________________

7. What do you like most about being a rabbi? What do you like least? ______________________________

Additional questions:

MASTER #17

NAME ______________________________

[illegible]

 NAME ____________________

'A BINTEL BRIEF': ALL ABOUT WORKING

1908
Esteemed Editor,

We were sitting in the shop and working when the boss came over to one of us and said, "You ruined the work: you'll have to pay for it." The worker answered that it wasn't his fault, that he had given out the work in perfect condition. "You're trying to tell me!" The boss got mad and began to shout. "I pay your wages and you answer back, you dog! I should have thrown you out of my shop long ago."

The worker trembled, his face got whiter. When the boss noticed how his face paled, he gestured, spat and walked away. The worker said no more. Tired, and overcome with shame, he turned back to his work and later he exclaimed, "For six years I've been working here like a slave, and he tells me. 'You dog, I'll throw you out!' I wanted to pick up an iron and smash his head in, but I saw before me my wife and five children who want to eat!"

Obviously, the offended man felt he had done wrong in not standing up for his honor as a worker and human being. In the shop, the machines hummed, the irons thumped, and we could see the tears running down his cheeks.

Did this unfortunate man act correctly in remaining silent under the insults of the boss? Is the fact that he has a wife and children the reason for his slavery and refusal to defend himself? I hope you will answer my questions in the "Bintel Brief."

Respectfully,
A.P.

Answer:

The worker cannot help himself alone. There is no limit to what must be done for a piece of bread. One must bite his lips till they bleed, and keep silent when he is alone. But he must not remain alone. He must not remain silent. He must unite with his fellow workers and fight. To defend their honor as men, the workers must be well organized.

1. Would you have answered A.P. differently? What would your reply have been?
2. What protections does a worker have today when he or she is unemployed or has been threatened or harassed by an employer?
3. Why do you think poverty was so widespread among immigrant Jews?
4. What factors *kept* so many of these immigrants poor?
5. What difficulties confront recent Jewish immigrants, for example, Russian Jews?
6. What would you consider to be the *ideal* working conditions?

NAME ______________________________

'A BINTEL BRIEF': ALL ABOUT WORKING

1908
Esteemed Editor,

We were sitting in the shop and working when the boss came over to one of us and said, "You ruined the work: you'll have to pay for it." The worker answered that it wasn't his fault, that he had given out the work in perfect condition. "You're trying to tell me!" The boss got mad and began to shout. "I pay your wages and you answer back, you dog! I should have thrown you out of my shop long ago."

The worker trembled, his face got whiter. When the boss noticed how his face paled, he gestured, spat and walked away. The worker said no more. Tired, and overcome with shame, he turned back to his work and later he exclaimed, "For six years I've been working here like a slave, and he tells me, 'You dog, I'll throw you out!' I wanted to pick up an iron and smash his head in, but I saw before me my wife and five children who want to eat!"

Obviously, the offended man felt he had done wrong in not standing up for his honor as a worker and human being. In the shop, the machines hummed, the irons thumped, and we could see the tears running down his cheeks.

Did this unfortunate man act correctly in remaining silent under the insults of the boss? Is the fact that he has a wife and children the reason for his slavery and refusal to defend himself? I hope you will answer my questions in the "Bintel Brief."

Respectfully,
A.P.

Answer:

The worker cannot help himself alone. There is no limit to what must be done for a piece of bread. One must bite his lips till they bleed, and keep silent when he is alone. But he must not remain alone. He must not remain silent. He must unite with his fellow workers and fight. To defend their honor as men, the workers must be well organized.

1. Would you have answered A.P. differently? What would your reply have been?
2. What protections does a worker have today when he or she is unemployed or has been threatened or harassed by an employer?
3. Why do you think poverty was so widespread among immigrant Jews?
4. What factors kept so many of these immigrants poor?
5. What difficulties confront recent Jewish immigrants, for example, Russian Jews?
6. What would you consider to be the ideal working conditions?

MASTER #13 NAME ______________________________

 NAME ____________________

JEWISH ORGANIZATIONS

Many observers of Jewish history and the Jewish community in America today note that Jewish life has always been rich with organizations. Below is a list of some of the major Jewish organizations in America. How many do you know? To which do you and your family belong? What do the organizations do? At the bottom, there is space to write some of the activities offered by the organizations to which your family belongs and to write the names of other groups not listed here in which your family holds membership.

Agudath Israel of America
American Jewish Committee
American Jewish Congress
American Jewish Historical Society
American Jewish Joint Distribution Committee
American Red Magen David for Israel
American Society for Jewish Music
Anti-Defamation League of B'nai B'rith
B'nai B'rith
B'nai B'rith Youth Organization
Center For Holocaust Studies
Emunah Women of America
Federation of Jewish Philanthropies
Hadassah
Hebrew Culture Foundation
Hebrew Immigrant Aid Society (HIAS)
Jewish Chautauqua Society
Jewish Labor Committee
Jewish Labor Bund
Jewish War Veterans
Merkos L'inyonei Chinuch
National Conference on Soviet Jewry
National Council of Jewish Women
Pioneer Women
Student Struggle for Soviet Jewry
United Jewish Appeal
Women's American ORT
Workmen's Circle
Zionist Organization of America

NAME ______________________________

JEWISH ORGANIZATIONS

Many observers of Jewish history and the Jewish community in America today note that Jewish life has always been rich with organizations. Below is a list of some of the major Jewish organizations in America. How many do you know? To which do you and your family belong? What do the organizations do? At the bottom, there is space to write some of the activities offered by the organizations to which your family belongs and to write the names of other groups not listed here in which your family holds membership.

Agudath Israel of America
American Jewish Committee
American Jewish Congress
American Jewish Historical Society
American Jewish Joint Distribution Committee
American Red Magen David for Israel
American Society for Jewish Music
Anti-Defamation League of B'nai B'rith
B'nai B'rith
B'nai B'rith Youth Organization
Center For Holocaust Studies
Emunah Women of America
Federation of Jewish Philanthropies
Hadassah
Hebrew Culture Foundation

Hebrew Immigrant Aid Society (HIAS)
Jewish Chautauqua Society
Jewish Labor Committee
Jewish Labor Bund
Jewish War Veterans
Merkos L'inyonei Chinuch
National Conference on Soviet Jewry
National Council of Jewish Women
Pioneer Women
Student Struggle for Soviet Jewry
United Jewish Appeal
Women's American ORT
Workmen's Circle
Zionist Organization of America

____

____

____

____

____

____

____

____

____

____

MASTER #20 NAME ____________________

THE JEWISH WEDDING

Throughout the centuries, the Jewish wedding has been filled with a rich mixture of religious and cultural customs and religious objects, many of which are still part of the ceremony today. Describe each of the customs and objects listed below and briefly explain its role in the ceremony.

1. RITUAL BATH (*MIKVAH*) ____________________

2. WHITE ROBE (*KITTEL*) ____________________

3. CANOPY (*HUPPAH*) ____________________

4. SEVEN BENEDICTIONS (*SHEVA BRAKHOT*) ____________________

5. CUP OF WINE ____________________

6. WITNESSES ____________________

7. PLAIN RING ____________________

8. SMALL EMPTY GLASS ____________________

9. WEDDING FEAST (*SEUDAT MITZVAH*) ____________________

10. PRIVATE TIME (*YIHUD*) ____________________

NAME ______________________________

THE JEWISH WEDDING

Throughout the centuries, the Jewish wedding has been filled with a rich mixture of religious and cultural customs and religious objects, many of which are still part of the ceremony today. Describe each of the customs and objects listed below and briefly explain its role in the ceremony.

1. RITUAL BATH (MIKVAH) ______________________________

2. WHITE ROBE (KITTEL) ______________________________

3. CANOPY (HUPPAH) ______________________________

4. SEVEN BENEDICTIONS (SHEVA BRAKHOT) ______________________________

5. CUP OF WINE ______________________________

6. WITNESSES ______________________________

7. PLAIN RING ______________________________

8. SMALL EMPTY GLASS ______________________________

9. WEDDING FEAST (SEUDAT MITZVAH) ______________________________

10. PRIVATE TIME (YIHUD) ______________________________

 NAME ____________________

MATCHMAKER, MATCHMAKER

The matchmaker or *shadkhan* was a popular figure in the shtetls of Eastern Europe. Today, we still have matchmakers who bring young people together for the purpose of marriage.

Here is a letter on the subject written in 1930 to the *Jewish Daily Forward's* "A Bintel Brief."

1930

Worthy Editor,

A short time ago my friends and relatives discussed the role of the matchmaker in present-day society. The discussion arose in connection with my sister, a woman in her thirties who has been a widow for about ten years.

My sister had a good education in Europe. In America she graduated from high school and had two years of college. We in the family are proud of her because she is smart, well educated, and has a fine character. But it hurts us to see her wasting her best years alone. We would very much like to have her remarry. Since she is involved in business and seldom goes out, I expressed an opinion that she ought to go to a "shadkhan", who could easily arrange a match for her.

My sister answered that anyone with self-respect wouldn't go to a matchmaker, because that seemed to her like going on the slave market. Marriage to her means the union of two people bound by friendship and love.

Then a discussion developed on whether an intelligent, progressive person should go to a matchmaker. Some expressed the opinion that, when a person cannot find a match for himself, there's nothing wrong if he marries through a "shadkhan", since this is no obstacle to happiness.

Others agreed with my sister. They argued that going to a matchmaker was only for ignorant people in remote towns in Europe. A modern intelligent person should not go to be weighed and measured like a cow at the fair.

So we decided to leave it up to you, worthy editor. May educated, progressive people go to a "shadkhan"? We, and especially my sister, are very interested to hear your opinion.

With thanks and regards,
A Reader in the name of A Group

NAME ________________________________

MATCHMAKER, MATCHMAKER

The matchmaker or shadkhan was a popular figure in the shtetls of Eastern Europe. Today, we still have matchmakers who bring young people together for the purpose of marriage.

Here is a letter on the subject written in 1930 to the Jewish *Daily Forward's* "A Bintel Brief."

1930

Worthy Editor,

A short time ago my friends and relatives discussed the role of the matchmaker in present-day society. The discussion arose in connection with my sister, a woman in her thirties who has been a widow for about ten years.

My sister had a good education in Europe. In America she graduated from high school and had two years of college. We in the family are proud of her because she is smart, well educated, and has a fine character. But it hurts us to see her wasting her best years alone. We would very much like to have her remarry. Since she is involved in business and seldom goes out, I expressed an opinion that she ought to go to a "shadkhan", who could easily arrange a match for her.

My sister answered that anyone with self-respect wouldn't go to a matchmaker, because that seemed to her like going on the slave market. Marriage to her means the union of two people bound by friendship and love.

Then a discussion developed on whether an intelligent, progressive person should go to a matchmaker. Some expressed the opinion that, when a person cannot find a match for himself, there's nothing wrong if he marries through a "shadkhan", since this is no obstacle to happiness.

Others agreed with my sister. They argued that going to a matchmaker was only for ignorant people in remote towns in Europe. A modern intelligent person should not go to be weighed and measured like a cow at the fair.

So we decided to leave it up to you, worthy editor. May educated, progressive people go to a "shadkhan"? We, and especially my sister, are very interested to hear your opinion.

With thanks and regards,
A Reader in the name of A Group

MASTER #22 NAME ________________________________

HOW TO READ A JEWISH TOMBSTONE

NAME ________________________________

HOW TO READ A JEWISH TOMBSTONE

NAME ______________________________

HOW TO READ A JEWISH TOMBSTONE

 NAME ____________

ETHICAL WILLS

An ethical will is written by an individual in preparation for death. In a usual will, the contents deal with objects and money. In an ethical will, the contents deal with ideas and ideals.

Sam Levenson

Sam Levenson was a humorist. The major focus of his humor was the family–raising children and growing up in an urban environment. It has been said of his humor that it was of a special kind: it sought laughter at nobody's expense. This is his "Ethical Will and Testament to His Grandchildren, and to Children Everywhere."

I leave you my unpaid debts. They are my greatest assets. Everything I own—I owe:

1. To America I owe a debt for the opportunity it gave me to be free and to be me.
2. To my parents I owe America. They gave it to me and I leave it to you. Take good care of it.
3. To the biblical tradition I owe the belief that man does not live by bread alone, nor does he live alone at all. This is also the democratic tradition. Preserve it.
4. To the six million of my people and to the thirty million other humans who died because of man's inhumanity to man, I owe a vow that it must never happen again.
5. I leave you not everything I never had, but everything I had in my lifetime: a good family, respect for learning, compassion for my fellowman, and some four-letter words for all occasions: words like "help," "give," "care," "feel," and "love."

Love, my dear grandchildren, is easier to recommend than to define. I can tell you only that like those who came before you, you will surely know when love ain't; you will also know when mercy ain't and brotherhood ain't.

The millennium will come when all the "ain'ts" shall have become "ises" and all the "ises" shall be for all, even for those you don't like.

Finally, I leave you the years I should like to have lived so that I might possibly see whether *your* generation will bring more love and peace to the world than ours did. I not only hope you will. I pray that you will.

Grandpa Sam Levenson

Jack Riemer and Nathaniel Stampfer, eds. *Ethical Wills; A Modern Jewish Treasury*. New York: Schocken Books, 1983, pp. 192–193.

NAME ____________________

ETHICAL WILLS

An ethical will is written by an individual in preparation for death. In a usual will, the contents deal with objects and money. In an ethical will, the contents deal with ideas and ideals.

Sam Levenson

Sam Levenson was a humorist. The major focus of his humor was the family–raising children and growing up in an urban environment. It has been said of his humor that it was of a special kind: it sought laughter at nobody's expense. This is his "Ethical Will and Testament to His Grandchildren, and to Children Everywhere."

I leave you my unpaid debts. They are my greatest assets. Everything I own—I owe:

1. To America I owe a debt for the opportunity it gave me to be free and to be me.
2. To my parents I owe America. They gave it to me and I leave it to you. Take good care of it.
3. To the biblical tradition I owe the belief that man does not live by bread alone, nor does he live alone at all. This is also the democratic tradition. Preserve it.
4. To the six million of my people and to the thirty million other humans who died because of man's inhumanity to man, I owe a vow that it must never happen again.
5. I leave you not everything I never had, but everything I had in my lifetime: a good family, respect for learning, compassion for my fellowman, and some four-letter words for all occasions: words like "help," "give," "care," "feel," and "love."

Love, my dear grandchildren, is easier to recommend than to define. I can tell you only that like those who came before you, you will surely know when love ain't; you will also know when mercy ain't and brotherhood ain't.

The millennium will come when all the "ain'ts" shall have become "ises" and all the "ises" shall be for all, even for those you don't like.

Finally, I leave you the years I should like to have lived so that I might possibly see whether your generation will bring more love and peace to the world than ours did. I not only hope you will. I pray that you will.

Grandpa Sam Levenson

Jack Riemer and Nathaniel Stampfer, eds. *Ethical Wills: A Modern Jewish Treasury*. New York: Schocken Books, 1983, pp. 192–193.

YAD VASHEM
Martyrs' and Heroes'
Remembrance
Authority
P.O.B. 84 Jerusalem, Israel

דף־עד
עדות־בלאט
A Page of Testimony

יד ושם
אינסטיטוט צום אנדענק
פון אומקום און גבורה

THE MARTYRS' AND HEROES' REMEMBRANCE LAW, 5713—1953 determines in article No. 2 that — The task of YAD VASHEM is to gather into the homeland material regarding all those members of the Jewish people who laid down their lives, who fought and rebelled against the Nazi enemy and his collaborators, and to perpetuate their memory and that of the communities, organisations, and institutions which were destroyed because they were Jewish.	דאס געזעץ צום אנדענק פון אומקום און גבורה — יד־ושם, תשי״ג 1953 שטעלט פעסט אין פאראגראף נומ׳ 2: די אויפגאבע פון יד־ושם איז איינזאמלען אין היימלאנד דעם אנדענק פון אלע ייִדן, וואס זענען געפאלן, האבן זיך מוסר נפש געווען, געקעמפט און זיך אנטקעגנגעשטעלט דעם נאצישן שונא און זיינע ארויסהעלפער, און זיי אלעמען, די קהילות, די ארגאניזאציעס און אינסטיטוציעס, וועלכע זענען חרוב געווארן צוליב זייער אנגעהעריקייט צום ייִדישן פאלק — שטעלן א דענקמאל. (געזעץ־בוך נומ׳ 132, י״ז אלול תשי״ג, 28.8.1953)
בילד Photo	Family name * — .1 פאמיליע־נאמען * First Name (maiden name) — .2 פארנאמען (פאמיליע־נאמען פאר דער חתונה) Place of birth (town, country) — .4 ארט פון געבורט (שטאט, לאנד) | Date of birth — .3 געבורטס־דאטע Name of mother — .6 נאמען פון מוטער | Name of father — .5 נאמען פון פאטער

Name of spouse (if a wife, add maiden name) — .7 נאמען פון מאן אדער פון פרוי און איר מיידלשע־פאמיליע

Place of residence before the war — .8 סטאבילער וואוינארט

Places of residence during the war — .9 וואוינערטער בעת דער מלחמה

Circumstances of death (place, date, etc.) — .10 ארט, צייט און אומשטענדן פון טויט

I, the undersigned ______________________ איך, דער אונטערגעשריבענער

residing at (full address) ______________________ (פולער אדרעס) וואס וואוינט

relationship to deceased ______________________ קרובישאפט

hereby declare that this testimony is correct to the best of my knowledge.
דערקלער דערמיט, אז די עדות וואס איך האב דא איבערגעגעבן,
מיט אלע פרטים, איז א ריכטיקע לויט מיין בעסטען וויסן.

Place and date ______________ ארט און דאטע   Signature   אונטערשריפט

״...ונתתי להם בביתי ובחומותי יד ושם...אשר לא יכרת״ ישעיהו נו ה
"...even unto them will I give in mine house and within my walls a place and a name...that shall not be cut off." Isaiah, LVI, 5

* ביטע אנשרייבן יעדן נאמען פון אומגעקומענעם אויף א באזונדער בלאט.
* *Please inscribe the name of each victim of the Holocaust on a separate form.*

YAD VASHEM

Martyrs' and Heroes' Remembrance Authority
P.O.B. 84 Jerusalem, Israel

A Page of Testimony

NAME ________________________________

FAMILY COAT OF ARMS

Most Jewish families do not have a family coat of arms. These were mainly issued by the monarch to noble families within the non-Jewish community. It was rare for a Jewish family to obtain such a seal. One famous exception is the Rothschild family, whose name itself indicated a family coat of arms. The name Rothschild actually means "red shield."

Create a coat of arms for your family. Think about yourself and your direct ancestors (parents, grandparents). Draw a picture, a design, or a symbol which represents your family. Your completed work will become your own family coat of arms.

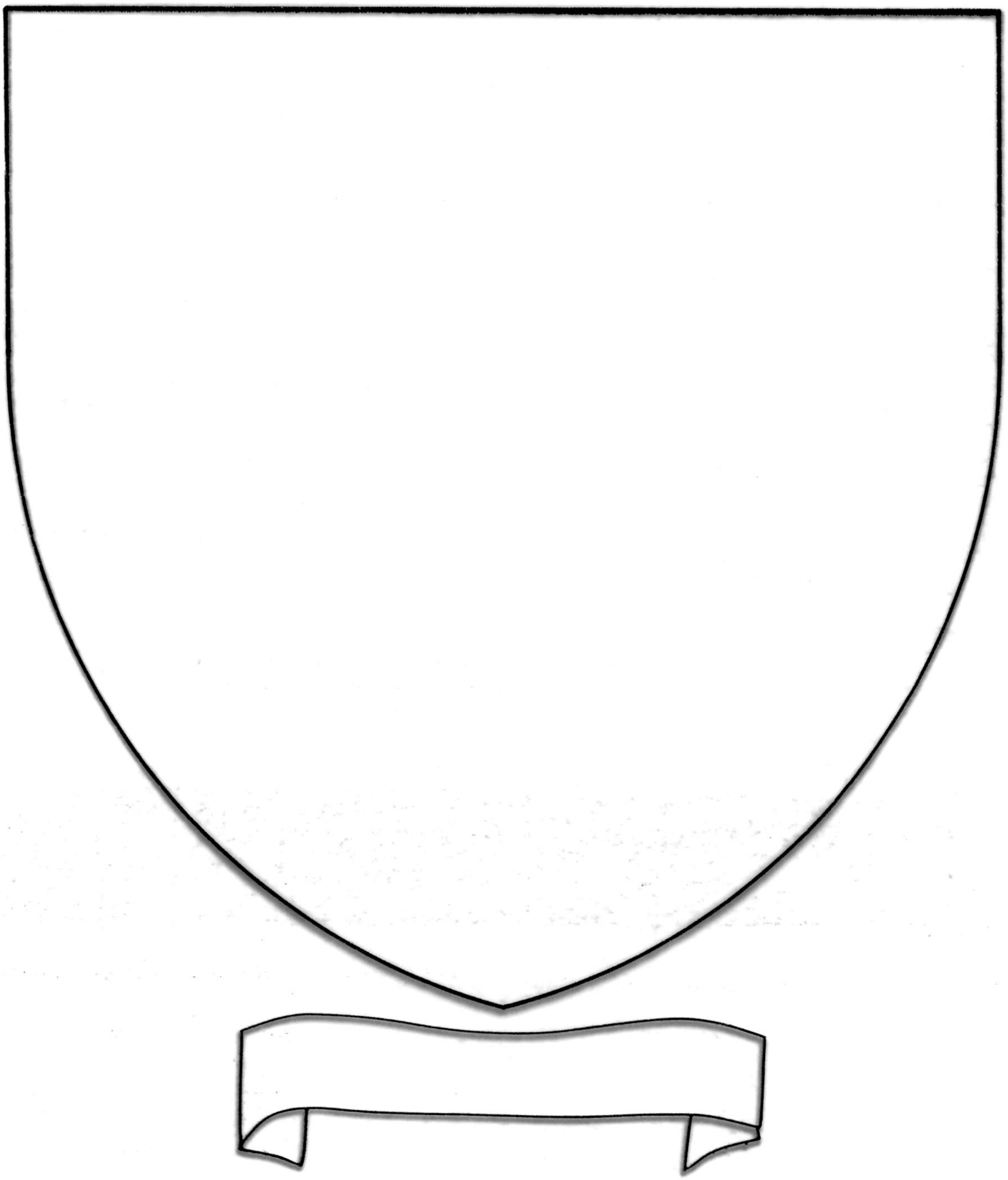

NAME ______________________________

FAMILY COAT OF ARMS

Most Jewish families do not have a family coat of arms. These were mainly issued by the monarch to noble families within the non-Jewish community. It was rare for a Jewish family to obtain such a seal. One famous exception is the Rothschild family, whose name itself indicated a family coat of arms. The name Rothschild actually means "red shield."

Create a coat of arms for your family. Think about yourself and your direct ancestors (parents, grandparents). Draw a picture, a design, or a symbol which represents your family. Your completed work will become your own family coat of arms.

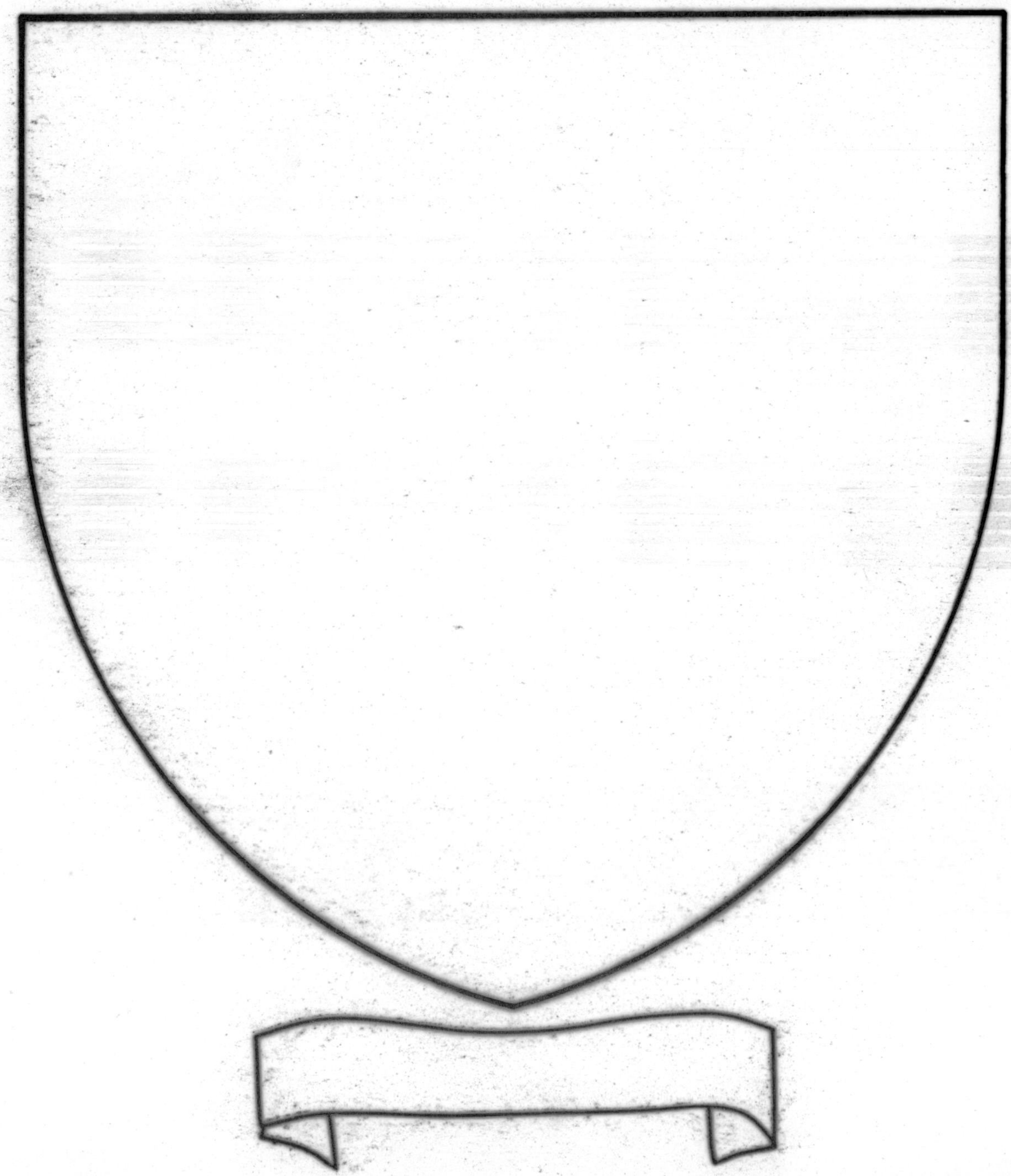